Praise for *Competing in*

"Li & Fung has been a pioneer in building and le[...]
the borderless world. This book reflects the wisdo[...]
succeed on the next global stage."
— **Kenichi Ohmae**, author of *The Borderless World* and *The Next Global Stage*

"The world may be flat but what does that mean for a corporation—new or
established—in operational terms? This book is full of insight into just that
question. It should be assigned reading to stir the imagination of corporate leaders
who want to get ahead before they find themselves behind. It's flat-out provocative
and flat-out good."
— **Greg Farrington**, Executive Director, California Academy of Sciences

"*Competing in a Flat World* integrates genuinely innovative thinking on network-
based structures with sound, established concepts in areas such as business planning
and accountability. By outlining the principles of network orchestration, the authors
provide a roadmap for successful change in an increasingly global environment."
— **Lennart S. Lindegren**, Retired Vice Chairman, Strategy,
PricewaterhouseCoopers, LLP

"We are led by unstoppable economic forces to connect our resources to form smart
networks, either wired or unwired. The authors bring forward the notion of
'network orchestration,' an almost one-size-fits-all strategy for organizations to
survive and excel in an ever-flattening world."
— **John Chen**, Sybase Chairman, CEO and President

"Properly orchestrated global networks are fundamental to the long-term success of
companies and their shareholders. Since this is a journey that may be longer than
the tenure of many CEOs, it is vital that boards and other top leaders recognize the
importance of network orchestration. This book offers a roadmap for navigating this
new 'flat world.'"
— **Dolf DiBiasio**, Retired Senior Director of McKinsey & Company and retired
Executive Vice President of Strategy and Investments at AOL/Time Warner

"For decades Li & Fung has been one of the most innovative companies in
reshaping itself to meet the opportunities of global business. Its model for network
orchestration has been one of Asia's best kept secrets. Now the secret is out."
— **Tan Sri (Dr) Francis Yeoh**, Group Managing Director, YTL Corporation

"To find your way in a flat world with no clear landmarks or well-worn paths, a
roadmap is essential. This book provides such a map for business leaders and is an
invaluable tool in today's competitive landscape."
— **Pat Harker**, President, University of Delaware

"In our own global business, we have learned to use partnerships to improve
performance, reduce costs, and build strong, innovative businesses. But global
networks are complex, and they require a different approach to management. This
book offers deep wisdom about orchestrating these networks and proven strategies
for success."
— **Paul Fribourg**, Chairman and CEO, Conti Group Companies

COMPETING IN A FLAT WORLD

COMPETING IN A FLAT WORLD

Building Enterprises for a Borderless World

VICTOR K. FUNG, WILLIAM K. FUNG,
AND YORAM (JERRY) WIND

Vice President, Publisher: Tim Moore
Associate Editor-in-Chief and Director of Marketing: Amy Neidlinger
Wharton Editor: Yoram (Jerry) Wind
Editorial Assistant: Pamela Boland
Development Editor: Russ Hall
Digital Marketing Manager: Julie Phifer
Publicist: Amy Fandrei
Marketing Coordinator: Megan Colvin
Cover Designer: John Barnett
Managing Editor: Gina Kanouse
Senior Project Editor: Kristy Hart
Copy Editor: Krista Hansing Editorial Services Inc.
Proofreader: Williams Woods Publishing
Senior Indexer: Cheryl Lenser
Senior Compositor: Gloria Schurick
Manufacturing Buyer: Dan Uhrig

© 2008 by Pearson Education, Inc.
Publishing as Wharton School Publishing
Upper Saddle River, New Jersey 07458

Wharton School Publishing offers excellent discounts on this book when ordered in quantity for bulk purchases or special sales. For more information, please contact U.S. Corporate and Government Sales, 1-800-382-3419, corpsales@pearsontechgroup.com. For sales outside the U.S., please contact International Sales at international@pearsoned.com.

Company and product names mentioned herein are the trademarks or registered trademarks of their respective owners.

Printed in the United States of America

Second Printing October, 2007

ISBN-10: 0-13-261818-4

ISBN-13: 978-0-13-261818-2

Pearson Education LTD.
Pearson Education Australia PTY, Limited.
Pearson Education Singapore, Pte. Ltd.
Pearson Education North Asia, Ltd.
Pearson Education Canada, Ltd.
Pearson Educatión de Mexico, S.A. de C.V.
Pearson Education—Japan
Pearson Education Malaysia, Pte. Ltd.

Library of Congress Cataloging-in-Publication Data is on file.

This product is printed digitally on demand. This book is the paperback version of an original hardcover bo

To our father, Fung Hon Chu,
who taught us loyalty and the value
of relationships.

Victor and William Fung

To Dina, John, and Lee,
who taught me the importance of
orchestrating empowered partners.

Jerry Wind

Contents

Acknowledgments

First of all, we are pleased to acknowledge the hard work of Chang Ka Mun and Helen Chin of the Li & Fung Research Centre for their extensive assistance with research and information throughout this process. We also are grateful to our many partners who helped us build this network and shared their insights for this book, including Bob Weinberg of KB Toys and Mike Mayo of Gymboree. We are thankful to many leaders within Li & Fung for sharing their stories and their own perspectives on both network orchestration and the Li & Fung business. We are particularly grateful for the involvement of Bruce Rockowitz, Henry Chan, Danny Lau and Fred Ip, as well as the contributions of Bob Adams, Marc Compagnon, Rick Darling, Dow Famulak, Tom Haugen, Albert Ip, Pak Chi Kin, Stewart Kwok, Alice Lai, Frank Leong, Irene Leong, Wai Ping Leung, Jasmine Lim, Emily Mak, Gerard Raymond, Alice Robinson, Ron Scholefield, Freda Tong, Allan Wong, Kitty Wong, Richard Yeung, Edward Yim, Angus Yiu, and Oscar Yiu.

Many colleagues and reviewers have helped us improve the book. In particular, Paul Kleindorfer, Colin Crook, Len Lindegren, Roy Carriker, and Marcus Pratini de Moraes actively engaged in exploring the frontiers of the "new theory of the firm" and made their mark upon this project in large and small ways throughout the process.

Without the consistent belief and guidance of Tim Moore at Wharton School Publishing, this book would never have emerged in its present form. We also have benefited from the active engagement and expert guidance of Russ Hall and Bob Wallace, as well as other reviewers. Our thanks also to Katherine Rohan for her great assistance and constructive comments on the manuscript.

Finally, we could not have developed this book without the involvement of Robert Gunther, who conducted interviews and wrote, edited, and collaborated with the authors in Hong Kong and Philadelphia through many iterations of the manuscript. We are very grateful for his many contributions to this work.

About the Authors

Dr. Victor K. Fung is Group Chairman of Li & Fung. He is Vice Chairman of the International Chamber of Commerce. He holds a Ph.D. from Harvard.

Dr. William K. Fung is Group Managing Director of Li & Fung. He has chaired the Hong Kong General Chamber of Commerce and the Hong Kong Exporters' Association. He holds an MBA from Harvard Business School.

Yoram (Jerry) Wind, the Lauder Professor and Professor of Marketing at The Wharton School, University of Pennsylvania, is an expert, consultant, and lecturer on business buying behavior, market segmentation, and marketing strategy. His books include *The Power of Impossible Thinking*. He holds a Ph.D. from Stanford University.

Preface

Competing Flat Out

As Thomas Friedman points out in *The World Is Flat*, a convergence of technology, globalization, and other forces has transformed the way we work. India, China, and other countries are an increasingly significant part of the global supply chain for manufacturing and services.[1] Geography, while not irrelevant, is no longer the obstacle it once was, and companies can stretch their manufacturing, customer service, and other business processes around the globe. This dispersion of the supply chain creates tremendous opportunities to change the way we do business in this world, and how we design and run our companies—if we are prepared to rise to this challenge.

Li & Fung has been working in this flat world since the early 1980s, long before it had a name, and now produces more than two billion pieces of apparel, toys and other consumer items every year. Li & Fung now accounts for more than US$8 billion in garments and consumer goods for some of the best brands in the world. By the time of its one-hundredth anniversary in 2006, Li & Fung had become the world's largest sourcing company, growing at a compound annual rate of 23 percent for the last 14 years.

Yet Li & Fung does not own a single factory. It is a flat business for a flat world. The company started as a trading broker in Guangzhou (Canton) in 1906 during the Qing Dynasty and transformed itself into a Hong Kong–based exporter and then into a multinational corporation. Finally, the company reinvented itself for the flat world in a new role, as a "network orchestrator."[2] It is now the orchestrator of a network of more that 8,300 suppliers served by more than 70 sourcing offices in more than 40 countries and territories. The company indirectly provides employment for more than two million people in its network of suppliers, but only less than half a percent of these are on Li & Fung's payroll.[3] With this lean structure, each of the company's own employees generates about US$1 million in sales, earning a return on equity of more than 38 percent per year. As a family firm at the intersection of the East and West, the company is both deeply traditional and thoroughly modern. Recognizing its creative thinking and use of technology, *Wired* magazine placed Li & Fung among young upstarts such as Google, Apple, and Amazon on its 2005 "Wired 40" list.

Over the years, Li & Fung's innovations have attracted attention, from business school case studies to magazine articles and books.[4] Now we are pleased to share more detailed insights from the transformations at the company and examine how they can help other enterprises to compete in a flat world. Victor and William Fung pioneered these transformations in the trading company founded by their grandfather, Mr. Fung Pak-liu. Wharton professor Jerry Wind has worked with them since 1998 on the company's triannual strategic review process and also offers broader perspectives from research and practice.

The flat world has ripped the lid off the corporation. It has broken through traditional national and organizational borders. It challenges the way we look at and run everything from enterprises to nations. Companies in manufacturing will find these innovations and shifts in thinking directly relevant. But the impact is not limited to manufacturing or to companies with offshore activities. The principles of network orchestration are relevant to any organization and industry (including services) that wants to take advantage of the opportunities presented by the forces flattening our world. The principles of network orchestration, discussed in this book, have applications in many areas, from managing strategic alliances (which have a poor track record of success) to services, to open innovation, to comarketing.[5]

As you read this, freighters and cargo planes are churning across the planet. High-speed information networks are whisking voice and information, and billions of dollars, instantaneously around the world. Looking down from the Li & Fung conference room on the thirty-fourth floor of Alexandra House, where we worked on the book, we could see the freighters steaming in and out of Hong Kong harbor. It is a hive of activity, and the pace of commerce just keeps increasing and evolving in new ways. Every day the view changes. It has been a tremendous adventure and education to have such a ringside seat on the emergence of this flat world and to be an active participant in its development.

These freighters are connecting points of the globe that have never been connected, in new and changing configurations. The ships and planes streaming across the world are rewiring the neural networks of commerce. How does your own thinking need to change to keep pace? Have you understood the implications of the flat world for your own business?

The flat world is here. Organizations that can embrace it and understand how it works will find that it offers many new opportunities. Those that cannot adapt quickly enough to these new realities will fall behind or be bought out by those that have learned how to compete in a flat world. The opportunities are as broad as the world. How do you need to remake your organization, management, and mindset to seize these opportunities?

Victor K. Fung

William K. Fung

Yoram (Jerry) Wind

1

The Orchestration Imperative

In the 1970s, The Limited began working with Li & Fung to source its clothing. To tighten the cycle time of its supply chains, chairman and CEO Les Wexner set a time limit of 30 days for any order to be produced. This was absolute, whether the order was for 5,000 or 200,000 pieces; it had to be done in 30 days. This was one of the ways Wexner pioneered the concept of quick-response manufacturing. To meet the tight deadline, it became a normal practice for Li & Fung to sample many factories and to have these factories ready before The Limited decided on the size of the order. In this way, Li & Fung could reserve enough production capacity to respond quickly. If the order turned out to be a big one, Li & Fung would use several factories to manufacture the item in parallel. For the production to look as if it was all done in one factory, Li & Fung had to control the raw materials, trims, and patterns for all the factories used.

But when the garments arrived in The Limited's distribution center in Columbus, Ohio, each box contained a single size, color, and style of shirt or other product. Upon arrival, the boxes were first unpacked and the shirts were placed on a shelf by size. Then warehouse staff picked them from the shelves, attached the right price tags and labels, and repacked the shirts into new boxes to provide the right assortments for each store. This was a process that sometimes took as long as two weeks, at U.S. wages. Manufacturers on the other side of the world were racing to get the products made in 30 days, but then the shirts spent as much time on the water and half as much time again waiting in the distribution center before they reached the stores and consumers.

The Limited and Li & Fung then worked out pioneering arrangements that changed the distribution chain. First, they frequently used airfreight. Second, and perhaps more important, instead of picking and packing the products for individual stores at the distribution center, they arranged for assortments to be created at the factory in Asia. As the shirts of different sizes and colors came off the line, they were packed into typical assortments and bar-coded (later the boxes used Radio Frequency Identification tags). The Limited also sent over its U.S. retail price tags, and factory workers put them on the garments before they left for the retailer's U.S. distribution center.

This meant that instead of taking two weeks to be picked and tagged in the distribution center, the boxes could go in one door and out another to smaller trucks headed to the stores. Cross-docking was born. The boxes from the factories arrived in stores, and the goods were put directly onto the racks. Shaving a few weeks off the process had huge implications in the time-sensitive fashion industry. Because of the bar-coding, the system even allowed for adjusting quantities on the fly. If there happened to be a particularly cold season in New England and a particularly hot one in Texas, more of the short-sleeve shirts could go south and fewer north. The cost of creating assortments and putting on price tags at the factory was much cheaper in Asia than in the U.S. distribution center because of both lower wages and a more streamlined process.

When Li & Fung originally proposed the idea of the factory putting on price tags, buyers at The Limited were concerned. How could a supplier be told the retail price (which was significantly higher than the manufacturing cost)? Wouldn't this lead to tougher bargaining and more demands from suppliers? This proved to be an unfounded concern. The competitive process of bidding among vendors ensured that prices remained low. Besides, suppliers already had a pretty good idea of what retailers were charging, and this information was easy to find anyway.

The concern about giving away information on price tags reflects the old adversarial view of the supply chain. Every part of the supply chain was wrestling with the other members. Supply chain members were engaged in a great struggle to see who could extract greater value from the chain. The buyer squeezed suppliers on prices. The suppliers shaved costs to boost their own margins. It was a fight for a limited pie.

The genius of Wexner of The Limited was his ability to see the bigger picture. Giving Li & Fung the price tags created an opportunity to make the entire chain more efficient for everyone. Wexner realized he was not competing against his suppliers. He was competing against other retailers with their own networks. To optimize the chain required a level of trust that was not part of the old thinking about supply chains. The old mindset was that each stage was separate and adversarial. This resulted in packing shirts in boxes and then unpacking them in Ohio. The new mindset allowed all the players in the chain to work together to optimize the entire chain.

> *Wexner realized he was not competing against his suppliers. He was competing against other retailers with their own networks.*

"Network orchestration" takes a broader view of the entire supply chain. The network orchestrator designs the overall supply chain, drawing together multiple factories in different regions to collaborate on a single product. Without orchestration, many of the gains of networks and global collaboration are lost because the resulting supply chains are suboptimized. What the discipline of management was to the old vertically integrated, hierarchical firm, network orchestration is to the company working in the flat world. It is an essential capability for this world, from orchestrating virtual networks such as Wikipedia and open-source software to delivering hard goods through global manufacturing.

The Challenge of Globalization 3.0

Thomas Friedman identified three primary periods of globalization. Globalization 1.0 might be seen as the rounding of the old flat world, from the time of Christopher Columbus's journey to the New World until around 1800. This was the emergence of a global market, with countries using advances in transportation and other technologies to connect with different parts of the world. The second period, Globalization 2.0, was the age of the rise of the multinational company, extending from 1800 to 2000. Falling transportation and communications costs drew the world more closely together and facilitated the development of a global economy. This age was driven by hardware revolutions, from railroads and steamships to telegraphs and telephones.

Today we have arrived at the third era of globalization, Globalization 3.0, the emergence of the flat world. Friedman describes this as the shrinking of the planet from "a size small to a size tiny." The most visible drivers of this phase are the *rise of the personal computer* and *the development of the Internet,* connecting individuals anywhere with each other (through e-mail) and information (through the World Wide Web) along high-speed fiber-optic cables. Friedman identified a third, less visible, driver of the flattening world, *workflow software.* These software programs allow individuals to collaborate on projects anywhere in the world, regardless of their location. This, in fact, allows dispersed individuals to work together to create a product or service—developing a cartoon program for television, delivering customer service, or producing 100,000 shirts for a retailer in New York in China or Guatemala (or both).

Friedman identifies other flatteners as well. The rise of *outsourcing* allowed companies to move their business processes to partners overseas, while *offshoring* resulted in a similar migration of manufacturing. The phenomenon of *uploading* allowed communities to contribute online to a collective product such as Wikipedia or open-source software. With *supply-chaining,* companies such as Wal-Mart began working with suppliers to improve their overall supply chains, cutting costs, streamlining logistics, and forging better links between suppliers and their own information systems. The next flattener, *insourcing,* saw the emergence of integrated logistics, as companies such as UPS took over more company functions than just delivery, from fixing laptops for Toshiba to delivering pizza dough for Papa John's. Similarly, the flattener *"in-forming"* put knowledge at the fingertips of everyone with access to Google—in other words, everyone. All of these forces have been accelerated by the *"steroids" of wireless, digital, and personal technologies*. These ten forces have leveled the playing field, connected the unconnected and flattened the world. This has opened up new markets for sourcing and selling, most notably in China and India.

This has led to what Friedman calls a "triple convergence": a critical mass of enabling technology, individuals, and organizations skilled enough to take advantage of these new platforms and the sudden arrival of more than three billion people from emerging economies onto this new, more level playing field. The world will never be the same again.[6]

Ripping the Roof Off the Factory

These forces have also ripped the roof off the factory. Since Henry Ford set up his famous assembly line near Detroit, the most efficient way to run a factory traditionally was to put everything under one roof. Then companies such as Toyota opened the front doors of the factory and put their suppliers just outside the gates. This created Toyota City. The suppliers were still geographically colocated on the same campus, but they were separate companies outside the factory. Companies such as Dell then engaged in global sourcing, purchasing computer chips and other technology from Asia.

As global logistics and coordination have improved, these suppliers can now be virtually anywhere. They do not have to be right outside the factory gates. In fact, "right outside" the factory gates now means anywhere on the planet. Boeing's 777 jet is assembled from three million parts from more than 900 suppliers in 17 countries around the world.[7] As Figure 1-1 shows, Boeing primarily produces the wings and fuselage, and assembles the aircraft (as shown in black in the figure). Most of the plane's components are outsourced around the globe. For its 787, the company is also outsourcing systems for collision avoidance and landing in zero visibility to Indian engineers at HCL Technologies outside New Delhi. This not only allows the company to find best-in-class providers for each component, but it also gives each of these nations a vested interest in the success of the aircraft. This, of course, helps in spreading risk and making global sales.

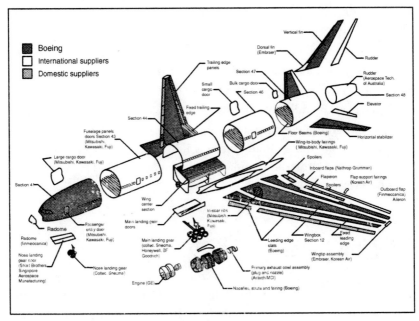

FIGURE 1-1   Boeing's global supply chain

Companies realized that the supply chain could be broken up and spread across the globe. They not only ripped the doors off the factory, but they ripped the roof off as well. They could do more than source *products or components* from other parts of the world. They could put stages of the supply chain in different parts of the world and coordinate them centrally. This meant breaking up the *processes* of the supply chain, farming them out to different companies in different locations, and then managing these dispersed processes. This is what John Hagel and John Seely Brown have referred to as "process orchestration."[5] A shirt could be designed in New York, be cut and assembled in Bangladesh with cotton woven in China, and be shipped to consumers in the United States. This was often the best way to optimize the overall supply chain to deliver the right product to the right place at the right time at the right price.

The modularization of the manufacturing process meant that different parts of the manufacturing process could be handled in pieces and coordinated across factories. Henry Ford's factory was built on the principle of division of labor. The new principle was *dispersion* of labor. Ford's factory was based on large operations that offered economies of scale, while orchestration was based on assembling armies of small and medium business that could act as one.

Dispersed manufacturing came to Hong Kong in the 1970s, when the rise of other Asian tigers made Hong Kong a less competitive location for manufacturing. For example, the transistor radio business migrated to Taiwan and Korea. At the same time, the reopening of China in 1979 after the death of Mao Zedong and the end of the "bamboo curtain" led to the creation of special economic zones in the south. Hong Kong companies could now send work to low-cost factories on the Chinese mainland for the labor-intensive parts of production. To compete with Taiwan, Hong Kong transistor radio manufacturers packed parts for radios into small kits, shipped them to the mainland for low-cost assembly, and returned the finished goods to Hong Kong for testing and inspection.

Similarly, 10-inch plastic molded dolls (such as Mattel's Barbie and Hasbro's GI Joe) became too expensive to make entirely in Hong Kong. The parts were molded in Hong Kong, whose factories had expertise in molding; shipped to the Chinese mainland, where they were assembled, painted, and clothed; and then were shipped back to Hong Kong for packaging. Eventually, as Chinese factories gained skills, the plastic molding and packaging were moved out of Hong Kong to the mainland.

Dispersed manufacturing is different from global sourcing. There have always been a set of suppliers that fed various inputs into the factory. Some of these suppliers, such as Johnson Controls, which makes entire interior assemblies for automobiles, have become very sophisticated and handle large pieces of the final assembly. But dispersed manufacturing is not just sourcing inputs, but rather spreading different parts of the manufacturing process around the world. For example, using global sourcing, doll clothing might have been bought from the Chinese mainland for dolls in Hong Kong. But the new model was not merely to import production inputs, but to move stages of the manufacturing *process* to the mainland. In effect, the factory started in Hong Kong, where the molding was completed; went to the Chinese mainland for assembly, painting, and clothing in different factories there; and then returned to Hong Kong for final packaging and export. No single factory was used; all of these partners acting together added up to a factory. This dispersed manufacturing requires designing the overall supply chain, optimizing it, and managing the processes across the chain. The new dispersed enterprise required a new skill: network orchestration.

When the systems were in place to move parts of the process to China, the process could be moved to almost anywhere in the world. The old under-one-roof factory was broken wide open. The world was the factory.

Increasing Flexibility: Precipitating Supply Chains from the Network

This dispersion of manufacturing processes is just part of the story of network orchestration. The other part is the network itself and how it builds flexibility. The modularization and dispersion of the manufacturing process has created further opportunities. Instead of a fixed network of suppliers, as shown in the Boeing example, the possibility now exists to interchange different suppliers to increase flexibility and responsiveness.

In network orchestration, the network is the universe of suppliers from which a given supply chain is precipitated, as illustrated in Figure 1-2. If an order for 100,000 dress shirts comes into Li & Fung today for a delivery date four months from now, the best set of suppliers for filling this order with the right quality in the right time frame will be drawn from the broader network. But if the same order comes in a month from now for the same delivery date, it likely will be delivered by a different supply chain that can respond faster. The world changes a lot in a month. Customer expectations change. Supplier capacity changes. The best supply chain for each given order will be created individually based on the order itself. Li & Fung's network of 8,300 suppliers stands ready like the famous Qin terra cotta soldiers that guard the emperor's grave in Xian. A specific supply chain is called forth in response to the demand of the customer. Henry Ford told his customers, "They can have any color they want as long as it is black," the modern network orchestrator can make a much simpler claim: "You can have almost anything you want. Just say the word, and the supply chain will be created. We will build you a virtual factory from a network of suppliers to meet your need."

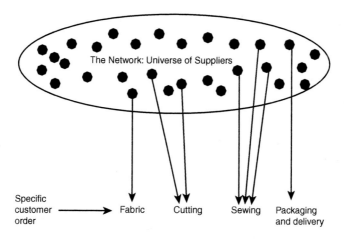

FIGURE 1-2   Networks and supply chains

The network orchestrator needs to think about building and managing this broader network, and also about designing the best supply chain from it to meet a specific customer need. In this sense, the network represents capacity, or potential energy. The supply chain harnesses that potential for a specific task. Network orchestration is concerned with both developing and managing the network, and designing and man-aging specific supply chains through this network. This is a new capacity that is essential for the dispersed enterprises of a flat world.

Network orchestration is concerned with both developing and managing the network, and design-ing and managing specific supply chains through this network.

Network Orchestration in Action

On May 30, a U.S. retailer places an order with Li & Fung for 300,000 pairs of men's twill cargo shorts. Li & Fung owns no factories, no weaving machines, no dye, no cloth, no zippers. It does not directly employ a single seamstress. Yet one month later, the order is shipped. In a flat world, the buttons come from China; the zippers come from Japan; the yarn is spun in Pakistan, and woven into fabric and dyed in China; and the garment is sewn together in Bangladesh. Because the customer needs quick delivery, the order is divided among three factories. Yet every pair of shorts has to look as if it were made in one factory.

If the order had come in two weeks later, it would have resulted in a completely different supply chain, using different partners drawn from a network of 8,300 suppliers around the globe. Like a message routed through the Internet, the project moves along the best specific path chosen from a broader network (see Figure 1-3). The supply chain is evoked by the order from the customer. This is the power of network orchestration.

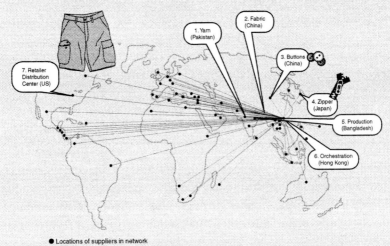

● Locations of suppliers in network

FIGURE 1-3   Traveling cargo pants

Orchestration: Most Evident in Its Absence

The need for network orchestration can be seen most clearly in its absence, in the failures of offshoring, outsourcing, and strategic alliances. Several recent studies have concluded that half the organizations that shifted processes offshore failed to generate the financial returns they had anticipated.[9] A study by Deloitte Consulting found that major stumbling blocks include governance, management attention, and change management.[10] Companies have also turned to alliances, mergers, and acquisitions to achieve global reach and growth, with worldwide deal flow reaching $2.7 trillion in 2005. But studies have found that only about 40 percent of all mergers and acquisitions (M&A) deals are successful in achieving their goals. (Some estimates put the figure as low as 25 percent.) Strategic alliances are also fraught with risks, with almost half of them failing. Culture and integration issues are a big part of the problem, so success rates can be improved significantly by having a dedicated alliance function within the firm.[11]

> *The need for network orchestration can be seen most clearly in the failures of offshoring, outsourcing, and strategic alliances.*

One of the primary reasons global outsourcing and offshoring, as well as acquisitions and alliances, often fall short of their potential is that managers have not recognized the importance of orchestration. This is the missing piece of the puzzle. It is different from managing a typical internal process. It requires a more fluid approach that empowers partners and employees, yet demands that control be maintained at the same time.

Networks need orchestration. In spite of the mythology, networked enterprises are not grassroots democracies, as they are sometimes portrayed. They are very different from the enterprises of the past, but when they work well, they have a structure and governance that, while distinctive, is rigorous. These networked enterprises do not just run themselves. They are designed and managed through network orchestration.

For example, although Wikipedia is democratic, it is not a completely open playing field. A network of some 13,000 writers and editors keep an eye on entries to ensure that they are kept current and accurate. Editors weed out nonsense pages, prevent the malicious rewriting of history, and ensure continued development. The architecture of the community, which often is forgotten in celebrating its populist origins, is largely responsible for ensuring that Wikipedia and other open-source projects don't disintegrate into chaos. Active orchestration of this network seeks to ensure that it produces something of value.

A core set of Wikipedia entries has been "protected" so they no longer follow the celebrated "anyone can edit" policy. These entries, such as "Albert Einstein," "George W. Bush," and "Adolph Hitler," were particularly susceptible to vandalism or "drive-by nonsense," in the words of founder Jimmy Wales. A 14-member arbitration committee also serves as the court of last resort for disputes about entries. Founder Jimmy Wales ultimately has the last word on difficult issues.[12] For open-source software collaborations such as Linux, a governing body ensures tight oversight and control of the work of the diffused community of programmers.

The success of the community depends upon its design, its governance, and the processes around which it is organized. Wikipedia has no autocratic CEO, but it has a system for generating and vetting entries that helps to improve the network and ensure that it operates according to a set of core principles. In a supply network, this role of governance and design is played by the network orchestrator. The orchestrator ensures that the collective wisdom of the crowd is tapped and that the network thinks and acts more wisely than any individual member.

Social networks such as MySpace and YouTube, on the other hand, which are less designed to produce a collective product, have less of a need for this governance and orchestration. They are channels and marketplaces, facilitating interactions or transactions. They are valuable in their own right, but because they are focused less on creating a collective deliverable from the network, they have less need for network orchestration. Manufacturing, on the other hand, is at the other extreme. Orchestration is essential. Otherwise, how can you be sure to turn out 100,000 perfect shirts at the end of the line?

Li & Fung is a network orchestrator in its purest form. The company owns no factories, no needles, and employs no factory workers. Other networked companies might modify this approach to their own needs. But where there is a network, there is a need for network orchestration. Someone has to play the role of orchestrator in the flat world. It could be the company itself, its partners, or an outside orchestrator. This role of designer and manager of the network is a new role and a new capability, which is often overlooked. But it is perhaps the most important capability for competing in a flat world.

The Broad Opportunities for Orchestration

Although this book focuses primarily on manufacturing networks, with which we have the most experience, the principles of network orchestration have broad applications across diverse industries and activities, from research and development to services. While Boeing was breaking up its manufacturing supply chain for building aircraft and dispersing it across the world, as previously discussed, innovative airline carriers were engaged in outsourcing processes and resources to transform their offerings. Before deregulation in the late 1980s, major airlines were asset-intensive. They owned their aircrafts, reservation systems, maintenance teams, baggage crews, and catering services. Upstarts such as Southwest, and later JetBlue and RyanAir, put most of their operations out to bid. They leased engines, leased aircraft, and contracted for baggage handling and maintenance crews. They retained the core of branding and the overall concept for the airline. This enabled them to cut costs and offer a very different positioning than the majors. But quality and safety still had to be maintained, and this required skill in orchestrating these networks to ensure the planes could fly on time and maintain their safety records even when the contributing business processes were not fully owned by the carrier. While the success of Southwest and other carriers is rightfully attributed to their distinctive strategic positioning, this positioning depended upon skills in network orchestration. The major airlines have now moved to more leasing and outsourcing as well. (For example, American spun off its Sabre reservation system and

Lufthansa spun off its maintenance operations as a separate firm.) Network orchestration is now a key capability for success in the airline industry.

We consider some other applications of network orchestration in Chapter 12, "Practice: A Lever to Move the World." These include the network Olam International built, working with small and mid-sized farmers in 40 countries to orchestrate a network for agricultural products and food ingredients. Other research networks, such as the Connect & Develop networks created by Procter & Gamble, have linked it with more than 1.5 million independent researchers around the globe; external networks have helped Canadian-based GoldCorp significantly improve the yield of its mining business by orchestrating an eclectic group of experts outside the firm.

Companies have created marketing networks to orchestrate hundreds of thousands of buzz agents to convey messages and promote products. Networks have been created for innovation, such as the system built around Nike and iPod to create an electronic personal trainer. Global sports leagues offer another example of the power of coordinated networks. Even the military is increasingly turning to networked models to meet the complex challenge of fighting modern wars and addressing global terrorist networks.

All these examples share one thing in common: They all are based on networks that come together to create a product or service. And they all require some form of orchestration to keep these networks from devolving into chaos. The principles of network orchestration can be applied to these networked enterprises in addition to supply chains and manufacturing.

Although Li & Fung is a large multinational, the opportunities for network orchestration are not limited to large global companies. These opportunities apply equally to companies large and small. In Hong Kong alone, at least 50,000 smaller trading companies manage global (or, at least, regional) supply chains. They all do network orchestration like Li & Fung. In fact, the new technologies and other shifts of the flat world lead to a leveling of the playing field that makes it easier for small firms to participate in networks or to engage in network orchestration.

The Three Roles of Network Orchestration

The dispersed factory is a different type of factory floor than the one Peter Drucker found himself on when he did his famous studies of management at General Motors. The management needed for these fixed factories is different from what is needed for these fluid, global networks. In the flat world, the traditional principles of management need to be augmented with skills in network orchestration.

What do network orchestrators do? The network orchestrator plays three primary roles related to the focus, management, and value creation of the firm or network, as Figure 1-4 shows. Each of these roles is the expansion of the role of a manager within a more limited fixed factory or traditional firm.

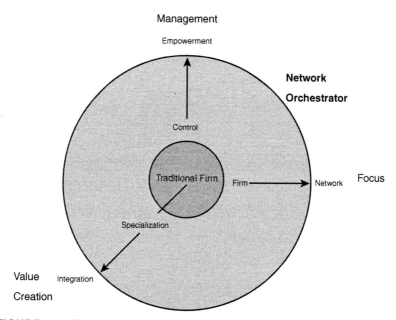

FIGURE 1-4 The movement from a traditional firm toward a network orchestrator requires a shift in focus from the firm to the network, a shift in management from control to empowerment, and a shift in value creation from specialization to integration. Because few companies are "pure" network orchestrators, and because the world is not completely flat, companies typically need to strike a balance somewhere between the inner circle and the outer one.

Role #1: Design and Manage Networks

First, the network orchestrator needs to shift from viewing the firm as the center of the universe to looking at the network. Companies don't compete against other companies. Networks compete against networks. Two retail stores on opposite corners in New York City might appear to be direct competitors, but this is an illusion. They are not competing against each other in isolation. Each store has a supply chain stretching from its shelves out to the world. The best supply chain will win. Before a customer walks into the store, often the game is over based on the superior supply chain. The best supply chain is drawn from a robust universe of suppliers. It is no longer possible to compete by looking at a company in isolation from the network. The network orchestrator also establishes the values and culture of the network, developing its guiding principles while absorbing the best wisdom and practices from the network itself. The orchestrator creates the broader network and then draws supply chains from it.

Role #2: Control through Empowerment

Second, in a world in which orchestrators do not own the means of production, they need a different form of leadership and control. A dispersed global network can devolve into chaos. What holds this network together? In contrast to rigid control systems used to manage factories, the network orchestrator relies not just on rewards, but also upon a combination of empowerment and trust, as well as training and certification, to manage a network that it does not own. In addition, it empowers its own managers and suppliers to act entrepreneurially. In contrast to command and control systems, the orchestrator works like a guest conductor in an orchestra. The conductor might not have the ability to hire or fire people, but he or she coordinates a highly skilled set of independent musicians.

Role #3: Create Value through Integration

Finally, orchestrators have a different way of creating value. Value in the traditional firm came from specialization, honing skills in specific areas, protecting trade secrets, and keeping out rivals and even partners. Value came from fighting for a piece of a limited pie and protecting specialized core competencies. Value in the flat world, in contrast, comes from integration, bridging borders as well as leveraging the company's value and intellectual property across the network. This integration also means spanning borders between functions within the company, such as looking to manufacturing in developing markets to identify new opportunities for marketing and sales. Orchestrators need to know when to open the doors wide to create value as integrators and when to produce value by focusing on the specialized resources of the firm.

The three roles of orchestrators are interconnected and work together. The more dispersed networks become, the more there is a need for empowerment rather than direct control. The more empowerment is given to suppliers and customers, the more managers need to look across the network rather than focusing on their own firms. The more organizations move toward orchestration, the more they need to be able to build and capture value across the network rather than within the firm. Together, these three roles move companies from the center circle of the figure to the broader outer circle of the networked enterprise.

A Multiplier

Network orchestration is a multiplier that increases the reach and effectiveness of the organization. It is not a replacement for sound planning and control processes that multinational corporations currently use. These processes are still needed within the organization, and some of them do not have to be changed dramatically for a networked world. Network orchestration extends standard business processes to a broader network, but also requires skills that are distinctive to network orchestration. By doing so, it magnifies the reach and impact of the organization, and increases its flexibility.

This broader network allows the firm to connect to the capabilities it needs (or those its customers need), wherever they are in the world. Whereas competitive advantage once was defined largely by the capabilities the company directly developed and owned, now it depends on the capabilities inside as well as those capabilities outside that the company can connect to. But to connect to these outside resources and capabilities efficiently and effectively, the firm needs a new capability: network orchestration.

Bumps, Mountains, and Superhighways: The Need for Balance

The world is not completely flat. In our rush to understand and embrace this flat world, we need to recognize that we live in a world that is flat and round, modern and ancient. Global trade regulations, national laws, trading blocs, and other factors add to the lumpiness of the world. Although businesses operate as members of networks, they are incorporated as independent firms, so there is always a balance between the view of network orchestration in the outer circle and the firm view in the center. Sometimes it might make the most sense to take a firm-centric view; other times it is best to look at the network. Controls might be needed in some areas, while empowerment is needed in others. Value can be created through specialization as well as integration. The flat world creates opportunities for greater orchestration, yet there are still opportunities for more traditional approaches.

One of the most significant sources of lumpiness in the flat world is the result of national trade regulations. Different countries create regulations to gain advantage or protect local industries, goals that they feel cannot be achieved through open markets. They create restrictions and import barriers designed to slow the flattening of the world and position their countries to advantage. Favorable trade status is given to certain countries, creating expressways that ease the flow of goods. Others are punished with trade barriers. Some of these have nothing to do with trade, but are a byproduct of geopolitical objectives.

Decisions about the shape of the network change with each new ruling by the World Trade Organization (WTO), each new bilateral trade agreement, and each new protective regulation. Today the political geography can shift very quickly to protect domestic markets or reward allies. The contours of the world can change overnight. This makes markets less efficient, and it makes orchestration all the more important. Network orchestrators can monitor the bumps, look for the superhighways, recognize how they are changing, and find the most efficient way through these changes as early as possible.

Another set of lumps in this flat world has to do with the risks of interlinked systems, from currency to political risks. These risks need to be assessed and managed, and they can reshape the playing field for business, adding to the lumpiness of the terrain. Natural disasters, currency risks, political instability, terrorism, local wars, and environmental issues such as global warming also add to the risks and lumpiness of the world.

Other lumps in the flat world for business are a result of the relationships and trust that are necessary in doing business. Transactions can be digitized, but trust cannot. It can be useful to consider why an exchange such as Alibaba.com, the leading online marketplace in China, has not taken over the entire market, as had been predicted. Like the online bank Wingspan, business-to-business marketplace, VerticalNet, or the online shopping service WebVan, which rose and fell during the dot-com bubble in the United States, this type of efficient exchange would appear to be unstoppable. In a completely flat world, this might be true. These sites promise much more efficient transactions without the cost of a middleman. What they lack, however, is orchestration and a recognition of the diversity of customer segments. Not all customers are motivated only by one-off or short-term efficiency and cost. In a world of lumpy relationships and bumpy national regulations, there is a need for something more than a platform for transactions.

One of the roles of the network orchestrator is to balance the flat and round worlds. The orchestrator needs to come up with the best customer solution given the current terrain, and then adjust that solution when the landscape shifts tomorrow, as it will. The orchestrator needs to keep one eye on the possibilities of the flat world and one eye on the very textured realities of the unflat world.

Not Where, but How

In the round world, the most important question in developing a supply chain or process chain was to determine *where* it would be handled. As in real estate, the rule was "location, location, location." The costs of moving goods around and tracking information were so high that geography was the first concern. Then the concern was "where to do." In the flat world, the first concern is "what to do." After the task is identified, companies can find the best place in the world to do it. This is a shift in thinking about business processes. By making this shift, managers can better leverage their own capabilities and tap into the global capabilities of partners wherever they are in the world.

A new concern arises: not just where and what, but also "how to do" something. How is the best possible way to get this particular job done? What is the best path through a network of global possibilities? The total quality movement within the factory focused not only on doing things right, but on doing the right thing. Similarly, the network orchestrator looks at more than cost and efficiency. The orchestrator focuses on designing the best possible processes across a global network for delivering the right product to the right place at the right time at the right price.

> *The orchestrator focuses on designing the best possible processes across a global network for delivering the right product to the right place at the right time at the right price.*

Orchestrate or Be Orchestrated

Orchestration is not a choice. It is an imperative. To remain competitive with partners who are skilled in network orchestration, companies have to be able to orchestrate. To enter global markets demands collaborating with local partners and orchestrating the business through complex networks and diverse cultures. In the flat world, a single firm will have a difficult time standing against a well orchestrated network. Yet managers at many established companies face a dilemma in moving to networked models. Their businesses and thinking are organized around a single firm. They are just beginning to think about sourcing from low-cost countries. They see the risks of moving to networked models—losing control over core parts of the business or sharing profits with partners. But they may not see the benefits. They don't have "the will to network." We hope that this book offers a clearer understanding of some of the benefits of networked models and the strategies Li & Fung has used to transform itself for a networked world.

Although we developed these insights at Li &Fung, the principles of network orchestration that we have honed in this context can be applied in many different industries and networks. If your company is part of a network, the question to ask is: Who is orchestrating? If there is no orchestrator, should you create or play this role? How can the principles of network orchestration—focusing on networks, managing through empowerment, and creating value through integration—be tailored to your own situation? If you don't see your company as part of a network, are you viewing your world too narrowly? Have competitors already created networks that are competing against you? Will you be able to survive in this world?

The following chapters examine how to compete in the flat world. Part I, "Focus: Firm and Network," examines network orchestration and the shift in perspective from the firm view to the network view. Part II, "Management: Control and Empowerment," explores the management needed for this environment, managing a supply chain that is not wholly owned in a world of greater demands for corporate social responsibility, empowering executives to act as entrepreneurs, creating stretch goals, building companies around the customer, and forging loose/tight relationships with networks of suppliers. Part III, "Value Creation: Specialization and Integration," considers how companies can capture more value by taking a more integrative view of their networks, as well as explores the need to draw together marketing and manufacturing to "sell to the source" in emerging markets. Part IV, "Implications for Policy and Practice," explores how government regulations—particularly trade barriers—are limiting the ability of companies to orchestrate and optimize global supply chains, and considers some of the broader implications for managers.

As Les Wexner found at The Limited, diffused supply chains can be optimized only through orchestration, by looking across the chain and abandoning the mindset of absolute control. Competing in a flat world means more than contracting with a company in Bangalore or Shanghai. It requires a different approach to the business. There is a need for new skills and a new mindset. The purpose of our book is to offer managers lessons about how to succeed in this flat world—not just how to build better supply chains, but how to build competencies in network orchestration and *change the shape of your thinking, strategies, and organizations* to embrace this flatter world.

Are You Ready for the Flat World?

- What are the opportunities for network orchestration in your industry?
- What network or networks is your organization part of, and how is the network used to create specific customer solutions?
- Which companies are filling each of the three roles of network orchestrators in your industry?
- Given the orchestration imperative, what should you do next?

Part I

Focus: Firm and Network

Business leaders need to balance a focus on managing their individual firms with a focus on orchestrating broader networks.

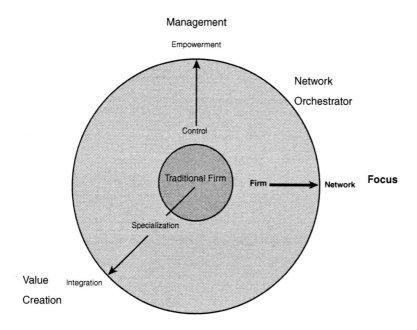

2

Orchestrate the Network

The flat world creates opportunities for managing the firm in the context of the network. This world also creates the need to build systems that are more flexible and customer-centric, which makes orchestration more important.

What is the power of network orchestration? In 2005, the youth lifestyle brand Ecko Unlimited was sourcing US$150 million garments from a buying office in Hong Kong using a traditional model. In spring 2006, in partnership with Li & Fung, the company moved to a network orchestration model. In one year, it reduced prices, improved on-time shipments, raised quality, and reduced lead times.

The shift allowed Ecko to create a strategic approach to sourcing. The company reduced its core vendors by 40 percent, to become more meaningful to these suppliers and improve monitoring, quality control, and communications. At the same time, the company tapped into Li & Fung's broader network to fill gaps in sourcing and respond quickly to new opportunities that required new vendors. Ecko consolidated the countries it sourced from while introducing new countries such as Indonesia to fill gaps. This more strategic approach to sourcing reduced average manufacturing costs by 15 percent in the first year.

The company moved its staff from Hong Kong to the countries of manufacturing. The local sourcing staff and quality control inspectors in the factories led to improvements in on-time shipments, which increased from 40 percent to 95 percent in just one year. Local decision making cut average lead times by 21 days, and quality also improved.

The Ecko brand has emerged as the touchstone of a generation without boundaries—with a fusion of designer, street, video game, and action sports that puts it in a class by itself. Now its supply chains also operate without boundaries and draw together the best of diverse vendors and countries to deliver better products faster and at lower cost.

What Is Network Orchestration?

As Ecko's experience shows, improved network orchestration can have a dramatic impact on sourcing performance. What is network orchestration? To understand network orchestration, it is useful to consider what it is not. Whereas Li & Fung does not own a single factory, global apparel manufacturer Esquel is at the other extreme.[13] It owns everything, right down to the cotton fields, spinning and weaving plants that produce the fiber, and yarns and fabric to feed its garment factories. It has a completely vertically integrated supply chain. In such a vertically integrated model, the need for network orchestration is minimal. The business is run by internal controls.

There might appear to be a compelling argument for keeping production under one roof in a single location: It provides control over the quality and processes of the entire chain. The ability to coordinate and control processes would appear to be easier within the walls of one factory. This is particularly true in a world in which social responsibility, workplace conditions, and environmental impact are increasingly important. As Andrew Carnegie said, put all your eggs in one basket and *watch that basket*. It also might seem that it would be less expensive to keep manufacturing in a tight geographic neighborhood. The costs of supervision, coordination, and logistics would appear to be much lower.

But in a flat world, this level of control can reduce flexibility. If new fabrics become more popular or trade restrictions change so the current locations of factories are less competitive, how can the company shift production? As consumer demand and cost structures change rapidly in many industries, there is a need for greater flexibility and responsiveness to customers.

Another model in the garment industry is offered by Luen Thai,[14] which has created "supply chain cities" in China where garment factories and other businesses are clustered in a single location. Like Toyota's supply chain city in automobiles, these concentrations of related businesses draw together manufacturers and suppliers in a single place. This model unbundles the vertically integrated firm further. Different companies manage different parts of the supply chain, so this is a step away from a wholly owned supply chain such as Esquel's. Buyers can fly to Luen Thai's locations and work out design and production at a single site. This model reduces logistics and coordination with customers and suppliers by keeping resources geographically clustered.

The orchestration model Li & Fung uses is very different from that of Esquel, Luen Thai, and a number of other vertically integrated manufacturers. As ownership is minimized, orchestration becomes more important.

What is ownership? Ownership is not as simple a concept as many managers think. It is not decided by lawyers or agreements. A fixed network of suppliers, even if they are not owned, can become de facto ownership as far as flexibility is concerned. If you purchase 100 percent of the output of a factory, does it matter whether you legally own the factory? You essentially own the factory and face almost the same challenges of ownership. (As we consider in Chapter 8, "Follow the 30/70 Rule to Create Loose-Tight Organizations," the strength of connections with suppliers must be balanced against the flexibility of the network.) The more the chain is built around orchestration instead of ownership, the more flexible it is and the more skills in orchestration are needed to manage it. Ownership means a commitment to fixed assets and investments, whereas orchestration is an asset-light model.

> *The more the chain is built around orchestration, the more asset-light and flexible the strategy can be— and the more skills in orchestration are needed to manage it.*

Most global companies are currently somewhere on this continuum between ownership and orchestration. They have moved parts of their manufacturing or service processes overseas. They have moved their call centers or programming outside the company. They have contracted with offshore manufacturers for production. (Even here, there are a range of approaches. Some companies such as GE have set up their own centers for outsourcing in India; others have contracted with companies such as Infosys.)

Esquel, Luen Thai, and Li & Fung all have created viable models for organizing supply chains to deliver garments and other products to global manufacturers. These models exist side by side and all can be used for different purposes. These diverse models do highlight differences in the balance between ownership and orchestration. Esquel represents the extreme of ownership and vertical integration. Li & Fung represents the extreme of orchestration. All three models require some degree of orchestration, but this need increases from the tightly owned enterprise of Esquel to the more loosely controlled networks of Li & Fung.

The Constraints of Ownership

From the viewpoint of the network orchestrator, the problem with ownership is that when you own your own production facilities, your concern becomes, to some extent, to utilize your capacity instead of answering a customer need. No business can survive without focusing some attention on meeting customer needs. But at the end of the day, an idle factory is a wasted investment. Payroll will be met only if the factory is filling orders. Staff and the investments in training will be lost if production is scaled back. Are you more focused on filling your capacity or serving customers? Ownership always limits the degrees of freedom in serving the customer in some small or large way. These fixed assets mean that the creation of supply chains has to start with the factory instead of the customer.

The network orchestrator turns this process on its head. It identifies a customer need and then builds a manufacturing supply chain or service value chain to meet this need. This is precisely the reverse of how the supply chain is typically developed. In fact, it is a "demand chain." The typical supply chain is designed to deliver some finished product or service into the waiting hands of the customer at the end of the line. The network orchestrator

> *When you own your own production facilities, your concern becomes, to some extent, utilizing your capacity instead of answering a customer need. The network orchestrator identifies a customer need and builds a manufacturing supply chain or service value chain to meet this need.*

starts with the customer and builds the chain to achieve the desired result. This approach breaks the tyranny of ownership and allows for greater flexibility in a global business environment that offers diverse pathways to meet these needs. As we examine in Chapter 7, "Build the Company Around the Customer," this allows the network orchestrator to build its entire organization around the customer. Orchestration models are more scalable, as Li & Fung's rapid growth and size have demonstrated. (Of course, the ownership discussed here is ownership of physical assets, not investments. A network orchestrator creates considerable wealth for its investors and value through the network without the fixed assets that might make it less flexible and less responsive to the changing needs of customers.)

Not every organization has the flexibility that Li & Fung has to completely reconfigure itself around the customer. Serving customers better leads to longer and broader relationships that benefit the business and avoid the very expensive churn that besets some companies. It is far more effective to hold on to existing customers and grow the business than to keep acquiring new ones.

At its root, the decline of the ownership model has been driven by the empowerment of end consumers. Consumers have more options and more power. As they have become more empowered (e.g., using search engines to find the best product at the best price), all the companies in the chain to serve them have had to become more responsive. Success now depends upon best answering the needs of the populous, and this means organizing around customers instead of the demands of the factory.

What Is "It"? Where Is "It"?

Online businesses such as eBay are adept at escaping the constraints of ownership. eBay does not own any of the millions of products on its site. Yet the company's online auctions and other businesses generated $6 billion in net revenue in 2006, a 31 percent increase over the preceding year.[15] With just 13,000 employees, this means that each employee generates more than $460,000. But the work of most of these employees is creating the platform. The real work is done by the more than 200 million registered users. eBay does not touch the products. It merely orchestrates the transactions between buyers and sellers, and creates a community where these transactions can happen.

As emphasized by eBay's advertising campaign, in which customers are shown purchasing a colorful "it" that could be any product, the company has built a system for delivering just about anything to anyone anywhere. This is something different than the supply chains of the past. There are supply chains for cars. There are supply chains for computers. There are supply chains for garments. These are highly specialized. But how do you think about a supply chain for "it"? The way to do this is to move from a focus on ownership to a focus on orchestration.

This is evident in a visit to eBay headquarters on the East Bay of San Francisco. Compared to the rich bazaar found on the eBay website, the headquarters is surprisingly subdued. Employees work in cubicles, large computers churn in the background, and the building has the obligatory Silicon Valley coffee bar. But where are all the electronics, automobiles, and obscure collectibles? Where are the garments and sporting equipment? Where is the "it"? It is nowhere to be seen.

eBay created a radically different view of retail. Just as manufacturing used to require owning a factory, retail always meant keeping inventory, with warehouses and stores. But the beauty of eBay is that the founders realized they did not need to *own* anything. No warehouses. No stores. This lack of ownership left customers free to build stores around their own needs, using searches. No one could have predicted what these "needs" might be, as founder Pierre Omidyar learned when he made his first online sale, a broken laser pointer, for $14.83. (It was not PEZ candy dispensers, as had been popularly reported.) The laser pointer was *broken,* but Omidyar found a buyer who collected *broken* laser pointers.

The entire business could be reorganized flexibly based on what customers wanted and what buyers had to sell. When enough sellers were selling something, eBay created a new category to make it easier for buyers to find it. The business is made possible by the emergence of partners for online payment such as PayPal (later acquired by eBay) and delivery partners such as UPS or the U.S. Postal Service. In this respect, eBay, which relies on a community of sellers, might have an advantage over Amazon, which has had to develop a network of warehouses. (In fact, Amazon itself realized a very lucrative business in turning its buyers into sellers, allowing them to sell their used books and other products online. It saw the value in moving from ownership to orchestration.)

In August 2006, eBay Motors sold its two millionth passenger vehicle, a blue 2005 Jeep Liberty purchased by a first-time buyer in South Carolina from a dealer in Florida.[16] eBay has been described as the world's biggest parking lot, where sellers can set up their tables for an online flea market. But it is much more than this. It has created a platform that allows buyers to confidently purchase cars they have never seen from sellers they have never met. This is no small feat. This platform includes buyer and seller ratings, and services such as financing, vehicle inspections, delivery, and buyer protection. eBay Motors was initiated by customers who began putting cars up on eBay, and the company then orchestrated this fledgling network, organizing it and creating the platform for it to grow and work productively.

Now imagine an eBay on which existing products are not merely bought and sold, but are *created* by the network. A customer asks for a dress shirt of a certain style and color, and the product is created and delivered by the network. This is the model of network orchestration. This is what Li & Fung does—not for individual customers with a single shirt, but for retailers placing an order for thousands or hundreds of thousands of shirts on behalf of their own customers.

> *Imagine an eBay on which existing products are not merely bought and sold, but are created by the network.*

The emergence of demand-driven value networks offers an escape from the constraints of ownership. The assets are not owned by the network orchestrator, which can begin with a clean slate in building the supply chain or demand chain for a given product or service. A shift occurs from "supply chain management," focusing on optimizing a fixed set of assets, to "network orchestration," focused on optimizing the response to a customer need using the assets of a network of partners. The customer thinks the thought, and the product is delivered. This is a completely different view of the supply chain and the customer. Obviously, constraints in the real world intrude between the ideal and the reality of this concept. But to the extent that these constraints can be removed or minimized, such as reducing the ownership of assets, the idea of a more responsive and fully customer-centric organization can be more clearly realized.

The Myth of Vertical Integration

Another challenge to ownership and a flaw in the vertical integration model is that true vertical integration does not exist. The ideal scale required for different stages of the process makes vertical integration impossible. One reason for this is the differences in capacity at different levels of the supply chain (as illustrated in Figure 2-1). The ideal scale for a sewing plant is less than 300 people, while dyeing, weaving, spinning, and producing raw materials (growing cotton) work best at larger scales. This means that many sewing shops will ultimately use the cotton from one producer. The result is that no supply chain is truly vertically integrated; certain parts of the chain will always be seeking outside buyers.

The dispersed supply chain recognizes this and allows the different parts of the supply chain to operate independently. The cotton growing and spinning are linked to a number of different weaving, dyeing, and sewing factories. Although these outside sales are treated as exceptions in the vertically integrated organization, they are the rule for dispersed manufacturing.

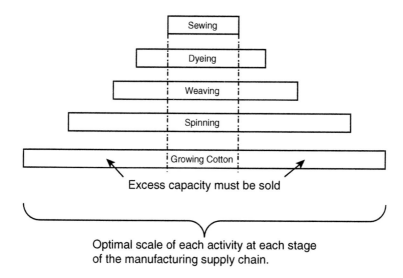

FIGURE 2-1   **Myth of vertical integration**

Global Dispersion: Why Tickle Me Elmo Wasn't Born in Manhattan

The vertically integrated factory or supply chain was created at a time when production resources were scarce. The capabilities for building automobiles were in Detroit. In some very specialized areas, only a few suppliers could fulfill certain needs. It made sense to own all of them. But today the capabilities are abundant. With the spread of management knowledge and technical expertise, these capabilities have been built in emerging markets. As Thomas Friedman points out, technology also makes it easier for small companies to act large and to collaborate with larger companies.[17]

This is evident in the toy industry. When he was a kid, Bob Weinberg, Senior Vice President of Merchandising and Product Development at KB Toys, accompanied his father to the Toy Center at 200 Fifth Avenue in New York City. His father was a sales rep in the toy industry, which, for a child, is probably the best job any father could have.

Until the early 1980s, the entire toy industry was centered in this one location. More than 95 percent of the U.S. toy business was transacted right there each year. The building on Fifth Avenue, erected in 1908 across from the famous Flatiron building, was so successful that it spilled over to 1107 Broadway. The two buildings, linked by a walkway spanning 24th Street, were known as the Toy Center. By the early 1980s, they generated rent revenues of more than $10 million, commanding a premium over already-sky-high New York City leases. Buyers from around the world came to a million square feet of wholesale space with more than 600 tenants. An estimated $4 billion in sales flowed through the center every year. This was the focal point of February's annual International Toy Fair, when 10,000 buyers descended on the Toy Center and the Javits Center uptown.

In 2005, 200 Fifth Avenue was sold for condominiums. It was the end of an era. "It was a sad moment," said Weinberg, who spent three decades in the industry with Toys "R" Us before joining KB. "It was a bit traumatic, but the business goes on. The best buying trips now are in Hong Kong in January," Weinberg said. "A lot can be accomplished there."

The same fate has befallen the New York City garment district, which produced 70 percent of U.S. women's garments and 40 percent of men's garments in the early 1900s. Production moved to the southern U.S. and then to Central America before migrating to Asia. Now the New York factories and showrooms are being converted into condos and Starbucks coffee shops. Although a lot of design still happens in New York City, design centers around the world and within factories address design at the production level.

> *In 2005, the Toy Center in New York City was sold for condominiums. In this world, you might not be able to corner the market on expertise or pin it down to a few buildings in New York. But you can find it all around the world. You can hire it. You can orchestrate it.*

Where did all these products go? Walk into the showrooms in the heart of the LiFung Tower in Hong Kong. It looks like a mini shopping mall, with the products of the company's major customers, including KB Toys, displayed in store windows. These "showrooms" serve as meeting rooms during customer visits, but they also demonstrate the breadth of production that has moved overseas, from toys to household products, to auto parts. Other showrooms in the company's larger apparel section are filled with diverse brands of shirts, jackets, and other garments.

But it would be a mistake to think that Hong Kong has become the new epicenter of these industries. There is no new Garment District or Toy Center. The capabilities for making toys and garments are not limited to a narrow geography. In a flat world, these capabilities have been dispersed. This means that owning the Toy Center on Fifth Avenue does not give you access to the world's toy-making expertise. Mattel's hit toy Tickle Me Elmo came out of a factory in Guanzhou that brought together capabilities for electronics and plush toys, working in collaboration with designers and other executives in the U.S.

In this world, you might not be able to corner the market on expertise or pin it down to a few buildings in New York. But you can find it all around the world. You can hire it. You can orchestrate it. You do not have to go to Detroit to design and build autos. You don't have to go to Silicon Valley to see what's next in technology (although it continues to be one center for this expertise). You don't have to go to Hollywood to make a blockbuster film. Centers of expertise do exist, but they are much more dispersed than they were in the past. This is, increasingly, a world without a center.

The Illusion of Trade Deficits

One of the great misunderstandings of global trade discussions is the focus on trade deficits. These discussions, often politically motivated, take the view that manufacturers in one country produce products, and consumers in another country buy the products. But the products sent out of Chinese factories to the United States are most often at the behest of a U.S. or European firm. Their supply chains could include stops in Thailand, India, or Guatemala, as well as China. The mistake is to imagine that one country makes and exports goods, and another country imports those goods.

This is the old world view. This is what Thomas Friedman calls Globalization 1.0 or maybe 2.0. It is a world of imports and exports. In the flat world, however, these goods and services are not merely sourced from a single country. They are produced in a dispersed manner in a number of countries. Dispersion is the true story of the flat world, and it changes everything we think about global exports and imports. What does a "country of origin" or a bilateral "trade deficit" mean in this world? How does this world challenge our current view of the firm, the design of the organization, and the primary responsibilities of managers? This is a new world, which requires new rules.

It is now possible to break up processes that were once within a single factory and disperse them across many countries without losing control over them. Although it is too early to say that geography is irrelevant—it is still important in many ways—it is becoming less important. This new reality changes the way managers need to think about their organizations and their work. Dell Computers might appear to be in Texas, but it has more employees working for it in Asia. Li & Fung looks to the world like a Hong Kong–based firm, but Hong Kong is the nexus of a fluid, borderless, pulsating global manufacturing enterprise spread over 40 countries.

> *What does a "country of origin" or a "trade deficit" mean in this world? This is a new world, which requires new rules.*

Importance of the Conductor

An outside observer might consider that the musicians do all the work in the orchestra or that the suppliers do all the work in the supply chain. From this point of view, the conductor waves his or her arms at the podium, or the network orchestrator merely puts buyer and seller together. But the network orchestrator, like the conductor, plays a critical role. For the conductor, the role is to lead and guide a very talented and creative orchestra to produce its finest work. For the orchestrator, the role is to lead a talented group of skilled and far-flung suppliers to produce their best products.

The orchestra conductor's success does not depend on talent with a particular instrument. The orchestrator's success does not depend on skill in executing a specific stage of the chain. An orchestra conductor might have skills in one or more instruments, but he or she usually does not play any instrument in the orchestra. The conductor's skill is conducting. Similarly, the network orchestrator might not be an expert in every stage of production, but has a deep knowledge of the overall process and how to assist expert partners handling a specific stage. The skill of the conductor or orchestrator lies in drawing out the talent and creativity of the network, coordinating all the individual elements, and ensuring the success of the overall process.

Just as the conductor draws together a talented group of musicians, the orchestrator assembles a strong network of suppliers, selects the individual musicians, and assigns parts for a particular piece. The orchestrator has several primary tasks, which have parallels to the orchestra conductor:

> *In the flat world, orchestration is one of the most important management skills. The skill of the orchestrator lies in drawing out the talent and creativity of the network, coordinating all the individual elements, and ensuring the success of the overall process.*

- The first is to design the process, to select the music to be played to please the audience or the products that will be produced to meet the needs of customers. The conductor is the musical director, selecting the music that the orchestra will play. Similarly, the network orchestrator selects the projects for the network and decides the best way to architect a supply chain for each project. Even this is not as straightforward as it may seem because the orchestrator needs to understand the audience and also demonstrate creativity in identifying opportunities for the customer.

- The second task is to determine which instruments will play which parts. This means both scoring the orchestral piece to determine what will be played where and also selecting the musicians. The orchestrator determines the supply chain needed for a given order, and then divides up the processes needed to achieve it and selects specific suppliers to fulfill those processes. The orchestrator also determines the critical knowledge and capabilities that need to be part of the network.

- Finally, the network orchestrator, like the conductor, stands at the front of the group and makes sure everyone stays in time and on the same page. The orchestrator makes sure each step of the process moves smoothly, uses its knowledge to address problems, and suggests solutions along the way. The orchestrator makes sure that the right product at the right price ends up in the retailer's stores at the right time. Given the relative independence and empowerment of the skilled musicians or suppliers, the authority of the conductor or orchestrator depends upon winning the respect of members of the network. As leader, the conductor also establishes the overall culture for the orchestra and articulates the values by which it operates. The conductor's baton is an instrument of coordination, not a bludgeon to force members into submission. Discontented musicians have been able to depose conductors who have lost respect. As with a democratically elected leader, the authority of the conductor or orchestrator is derived from those who follow.

Two Types of Networks: Fixed or Flexible

Networks have varying degrees of flexibility. Some, like the network Boeing has built in aircraft, discussed in Chapter 1, "The Orchestration Imperative," are more fixed networks. This resembles the standing orchestra, which works closely together over a long period of time to create a unique sound. Concert-goers talk about the "Philadelphia sound" of the Philadelphia Orchestra. Together the musicians create what Oliver Williamson calls "idiosyncratic investments" in the network.[18] This type of investment is common in the semiconductor, aerospace, and defense industries. It is difficult to get into such a network as a supplier, but for those who are in, the networks tend to be fairly stable because of the switching costs of bringing new partners up to speed. The network members rely upon one another for the distinctive capabilities that they have created together.

In contrast to standing orchestras, contract orchestras are more flexible arrangements. A contract orchestra is brought together for a single performance or short-term set of engagements. A larger network of musicians might be prequalified to be part of this orchestra, but the exact configuration of musicians brought together is determined by the specific music required to be played. This offers tremendous flexibility but can lead to a less distinctive sound. In some industries, such as apparel, idiosyncratic investments might be less important and various suppliers with a sufficient level of quality can be somewhat interchangeable. This means switching costs are much lower, but the role of the network orchestrator becomes more important. The orchestrator has to ensure that these different players all work together to create a coherent output.

One of the critical decisions of the network orchestrator is to determine what type of orchestra to design. Should it be a more fixed and permanent standing orchestra with its own "sound," or a more fluid and adaptable contract orchestra? The decision depends partly on the need for developing specialized skills distinctive to the network versus those that can transfer across many networks. It also depends on the flexibility and adaptability needed, which the more ad hoc contract orchestra enhances.

Sharing Economic Value

The network creates shared economic interests among its partners. How is the value that the network creates distributed? This is a critical question. For the network to be sustainable, the network orchestrator must give careful attention to how its members share the economic value. As we will discuss in Chapter 8, suppliers enjoy many benefits from participating un networks. In fact, because they are not captive or forced to be part of the network, benefits *must* exist for them to continue to participate.

In a free market, where small to medium-sized suppliers have other opportunities for selling their products and orchestrators have diverse suppliers they can turn to, the market itself determines a fair distribution of value. If a supplier's services are being commoditized, as with any business, managers must look for ways to develop value-added capabilities that give them more leverage in pricing.

But this free market is not always the case. A large retailer with a fixed set of suppliers dependent upon it for survival could use this power to squeeze suppliers to the point that their businesses are barely profitable or even unprofitable. For a large company, this temptation might be mitigated by reputational risk that could make it harder to attract partners in the future. Sustaining its business also depends upon the continued success of its suppliers, so a large player cannot be cavalier about the success and survival of the partners in its network. The network is a symbiotic relationship.

For the network to be sustainable, the network orchestrator must give careful attention to how its members share the economic value.

A more flexible network faces fewer problems of power imbalances and sharing value. The orchestrator does not purchase all the output of a given supplier, so the supplier is not captive. New technologies give smaller players a more level playing field, and allow them to access a broader range of potential partners and markets for their services from around the world. This flexibility benefits the suppliers but does not hurt the smart orchestrator.

A larger company does not always have the upper hand in such networks. In some cases, it might be difficult for a network orchestrator to switch from a supplier with very rare or specialized capabilities (as in semiconductors or very customized products). In this case, a critical smaller supplier could raise its prices. At a certain point, the higher prices will likely attract new competitors and open up the market, but in areas where it takes many years to build such capabilities, this could be a slow process, allowing the supplier to extract more value.

The relationship and shared value between large companies in the same network can be complex. For example, in aircraft, neither General Electric (which makes engines) nor Boeing would relinquish control over the networks or the value that is created. In this case, such a network might have "twin stars," with two orchestrators at the center. Orchestrators of subassemblies also might create a significant part of the final product. In this case, the primary network orchestrator is an orchestrator of orchestrators.

In some cases, the network is orchestrated and shaped by a combination of public and private forces. For example, in the 1980s, London's position as a major financial center was threatened to be eclipsed by the emergence of Frankfurt when the European Central Bank moved its offices there. London underwent its "Big Bang" deregulation in 1986, eliminating fixed commissions and enabling increased use of electronic systems. The changes resulted in a significant increase in financial business activities in London. Many of the merchant banks and their executives are not British. Now not only is the city seen as a major exchange in Europe, but the Big Bang set in motion a chain of events that connected London to the world and made it a major hub of global finance.

A Baton at the Front

No matter how the orchestra or network is configured and how value is shared, there is a need for orchestration. No orchestra would think of running without a conductor. No network should be left without an active and effective orchestrator. For small ensembles, one of the musicians often fills the role of the conductor. In a supply chain, a member of the chain or the retailer might fill the role of the orchestrator. Even so, this role of orchestration must be well understood and skillfully executed: The success of the overall process depends on it. In vertically integrated supply chains or other value chains, the owner of the chain is the orchestrator. Because everything is inside, orchestration reduces to traditional supply chain management. As the supply chain becomes more dispersed and more loosely linked, the management of the supply chain—and the supply network— becomes more complex. This creates an increasing need for orchestration.

The difference between traditional supply chain management and network orchestration is like the difference between producing a symphony on a computer, with all the inputs specified and controlled within the computer, and producing a symphony with a live orchestra. The computer-generated piece still involves great skill in specifying and coordinating all the tasks, but the tasks can be controlled more or less centrally. The live orchestra, on the other hand, depends upon the individual contributions of musicians, with their own strengths, weaknesses, temperaments, and positions in the orchestra.

Although every member of the orchestra is responsible for the success of a concert, the maestro is the one at the center who is ultimately credited with success or failure. Everyone in the network plays a part, but the orchestrator is responsible for delivering the right product to the right place at the right time at the right price. Whereas the musicians are responsible for their specific parts, the conductor is responsible for the whole.

Are You Ready for the Flat World?

- Are your supply or service value chains primarily owned or orchestrated?
- What are the opportunities of moving from ownership to more orchestration?
- Who are the network orchestrators in your markets?
- Would you be better served by a "standing orchestra" or a "contract orchestra" model?
- Given the rising need for network orchestration, what do you need to do next?

3

Compete Network Against Network

Companies used to see competition as firm against firm. But a networked world is like a team sport—the final score depends not on one player, but on the strength of the entire team. The best network will win. How do you design a network that provides a platform for rapid growth?

With the start of spring, the minds of all red-blooded males north of the Mason-Dixon Line in North America turn toward the barbecue. With the thawing of the snows, rolling out the barbecue is a ritual act of welcoming the summer. It is the modern equivalent of dancing around the maypole. Tossing steaks or burgers on the barbecue means the coming of summer. When the snow thaws, it triggers the barbecue reflex in the brain.

For manufacturers and retailers who sell these grills, spring is not such a happy time. This purchase pattern means that, at the beginning of May, all the customers for grills converge on retail stores at roughly the same moment. They all want their grills and want them now. Before this point, consumers are buying snow shovels. Then, like throwing a switch, they are buying grills. The result is that a product with almost no demand for much of the year is suddenly flying off the shelves. In a period of a few months, all the barbecues that will be sold are sold. For the factories in China that make these grills, this means nine months of not producing a single grill, followed by three months of working around the clock. This means finding enough workers, luring them back from the countryside, and then laying them off when the work stops. It means overtime pay, problems obtaining supplies, and shipping nightmares. It means sourcing gas nozzles from Italy and rolled steel from different parts of the world in sufficient quantities early enough to meet demand.

For retailers, it means nail-biting moments waiting for the shipments to arrive or paying extra for air shipping to make sure they do. The last thing the retailer wants is for a barbecue-obsessed customer to walk in the door and walk out empty-handed. It could mean more than losing a sale. It could mean losing a customer to a competitor.

The solution to this dilemma is actually quite simple. The factories can smooth out production of grills over a longer period of time and warehouse the grills. This avoids overtime and ensures a steady supply for the retailers. Your garden-variety barbecue is not like a luxury automobile or fashion dress. It does not change radically in design from year to year, so it can be designed and produced in advance without going out of style. But the complication is that this smoothing of production is not a solution that the factories can arrive at on their own. If they invest in warehousing, they have to bear the added cost and could be stuck with the product if they misread demand. The factories also have to carry the expense of the production and warehousing until they sell the grills to the retailers. With a stockpile of products in the warehouse, they could be susceptible to pricing pressure from retailers, who would then have the upper hand. So suppliers, on their own, cannot come up with a good solution to this challenge.

Neither can retailers, who want to keep their costs down and do not want to invest too much in the manufacturers' businesses. These investments could leave them vulnerable and put them at a disadvantage in negotiating with the suppliers. Left alone, both retailer and manufacturer will try to optimize their own businesses, with the result that the overall system is suboptimal. This is a problem that cannot be solved one piece at a time. It can be solved only by looking across the entire chain—including the retailer and manufacturer—and optimizing the entire network.

Working with a major North American retailer that sources $75 million worth of barbecues per year, Li & Fung essentially stretched out the production cycle. As the network orchestrator, it offered the factories 120-day credit terms on behalf of the retailers and arranged for warehousing the grills. Instead of starting production in October, the factory could start in the beginning of August, adding two months to the production cycle. This meant less overtime for the factory. Most of the shipping can be done by sea, reducing expenses and avoiding rush charges. The retailer received the barbecue grills at a little lower cost, even with the storage charges. The factory had fewer disruptions and lower costs. Both sides benefited because the overall supply chain was greatly improved.

> *Neither the suppliers nor the retailers can solve the problem of the spike in demand for barbecue grills without looking at the broader orchestration of the network.*

The New Competition

Competition is no longer company against company, but rather *supply chain against supply chain*. Partners in the chain are all members of the same team trying to optimize value. If the other chain kills your chain, all of you are out of business. The more the members of the supply chain *cooperate* with one another, the better they can *compete* with rivals. This is a different view of partnership and a broader view of the firm itself.

This changes the way members of the supply chain interact with one another. In the old supply chains (or other "value chains" that deliver products or services), suppliers tried to extract the best prices from buyers. Buyers sought concessions

> *Competition is no longer company against company, but rather supply chain against supply chain. This is a different view of partnership and a broader view of the firm itself.*

from suppliers. Each player optimized one piece of the chain. This leads to classic "bullwhip" effects, where lags in orders and lack of coordination lead to excess inventories or stockouts. The retailer without the right product on its shelves is at a disadvantage to rivals that have a better supply chain. Wild fluctuations in demand play havoc with factory production schedules.

In a European football (soccer) game, if individual players are always vying for control of the ball and scoring a goal, the entire team will lose against a more cooperative competitor. The individual skill of the players is important, but just as important is their ability to work together. A cooperative team of mediocre players will almost always outperform an uncooperative team of prima donnas. Studies of basketball, for example, find that the most successful teams are not those with one outstanding star player. Instead, the best teams are those that work smoothly together. This is the same with supply chains. A set of solid partners in a well-designed and well-coordinated network can outperform a star in one part of the chain with a weak team.

A study of rowers found a similar result. A crew team with the four strongest rowers was pitted against another team with less powerful competitors but better coordination. The coordinated team won the race. This is why these crew teams recognize the importance of carrying the extra weight of a coxswain to keep everyone in time. The coxswain, typically a very lightweight person, does not pull an oar or contribute to the forward motion of the craft, except for keeping all the other rowers in time. What does the coxswain do to justify bringing along this extra baggage when every pound counts? The coxswain does not row. The coxswain orchestrates.

> *In a crew race, the coxswain does not row. The coxswain orchestrates.*

Adversarial supply chains emerged because of a desire of each player in the chain to maximize its own efficiency and extract as much profit for itself as possible. An adversarial relationship can rarely produce the best results because the overall efficiency of the chain is usually sacrificed to optimize the returns for one powerful player. But much more than efficiency is involved in making a modern supply chain successful, and this is where the adversarial relationship can really be a detriment. Adversarial relationships dampen the creativity of suppliers, reduce flexibility, and suboptimize the entire chain in many ways. As flexibility becomes more important, the toll of this lack of coordination is growing.

Collaboration, on the other hand, can improve the overall supply chain. For example, consider rapid replenishment. All the Indian manufacturers of towels for a U.S. retailer are linked with the retailer. Using overseas collaborative replenishment, the retailer can cut inventories because it can track and count the inventories that are at the dock, on the water, and even in the factories in India. The manufacturers can keep some inventory of goods and yarns, and can, to some degree, speed up or slow down work in progress. Retailers never want to run out of towels, but now the inventory needed to deal with surges in demand can be across the entire chain rather than in the retailer's own warehouse. The retailer typically sends an EDI transmission to the manufacturer every Sunday night (electronically transmitting sales data); the manufacturer responds by Monday; and the needed shipments are on the way by Wednesday. This is a 72-hour cycle of replenishment. It truly has become a collaborative enterprise, with the entire chain working together to maximize results.

Improving the Network

A European retailer often complained that the orders of garments from a factory in Sri Lanka suffered from long delays. The Sri Lankan factory was excellent; the trouble was the fault of a supplier in Korea that provided the fabric. Although the Sri Lankan factory was among the largest in the country, its in-house sourcing department was small and had no staff or operations overseas. The raw materials were inspected when they arrived from Korea, but if the quality was poor and the fabric had to be rejected or exchanged, production and shipment were delayed. By the time this was recognized in Sri Lanka, the materials had taken a long and expensive boat ride. This added costs and delays, slowing delivery and increasing risks of stockouts or markdowns for the retailer.

The solution was for Li & Fung, acting as the network orchestrator, to inspect the fabric in Korea on behalf of the Sri Lankan supplier. This saved time and money. Except for its fabric inspection, the

Sri Lankan supplier had a very good factory. But what happened outside its factory walls turned out to be more important than what was going on in the factory. By improving the overall supply chain, the Sri Lankan factory had fewer rejected products and lower costs. The retailer had fewer delays. Looking more broadly at the entire supply chain and network led to tremendous overall improvements in the supply chain.

Many companies have begun to recognize the importance of a superior supply chain in competing against rivals. Companies such as Dell, Wal-Mart, and Toyota have designed supply chains that have set them apart from rivals and allowed them to deliver superior value to customers. Although some of these supply chains are based on flexible networks, they are often built around relationships with a fixed set of suppliers. The next challenge is to think beyond competing supply chain against supply chain, to think about competing network against network.

Competing network against network means that the companies with access to the best networks not only can outperform competitors today, but also have the capacity to flexibly outperform them tomorrow. They can create superior supply chains now and also design new supply chains drawn from their networks. This gives companies many more options in responding to customer needs. The best networks give birth to the best supply chains.

This is like the bench strength of an athletic team. While only a few players are on the field at a given time, many more are on the bench. Some players with certain skills can be switched out at different points in the game or if another player is injured or fatigued. In U.S. football, "special teams" are brought to the field for specific situations such as kicking a field goal or closing the last yard to the goal line. Similarly, supply chains can be drawn from a bench of good players and can be rearranged based on the capacity of the suppliers and the demands

> *A view of network against network means that the companies with access to the best networks not only can outperform competitors today, but also have the capacity to flexibly outperform them tomorrow. This is like the bench strength of an athletic team.*

of customers. Although not all the players are on the field, the team's ability to deal with whatever situation arises depends on the strength of the entire bench.

Competing network against network is much trickier than simply competing supply chain against supply chain. When partners in a single chain are shown the overall picture, they can see how everyone can benefit through cooperation. Being part of a network has its benefits, but these might be a little less clear, especially as individual members of the network are brought in for a specific project. Network orchestrators need to be able to make an argument for partners to be part of a specific supply chain, which typically is based on a measurable financial return, and also make a case for partners to be part of the network. Network participation is based on both tangible and intangible benefits, such as learning, trust, access to global clients, and long-term business development. Part of the role of the network orchestrator is to educate the entire supply chain about the benefits of working together as a team. (Of course, this is complicated by the fact that members can be part of more than one network, which sometimes compete.)

The Wisdom of Networks

As author James Surowiecki points out in his book *The Wisdom of Crowds*, a group can sometimes be smarter than its individual members.[19] This wisdom is seen in the success of Google's search engine, based on the searches of other users. As another example, although experts were correct only 65 percent of the time in answering questions from the game show *Who Wants to Be a Millionaire?* the "less expert" TV studio audience guessed right 91 percent of the time. Surowiecki points out that, "under the right circumstances, groups are remarkably intelligent, and are often smarter than the smartest people in them."[20]

Networks can also work "smarter" than the individuals or firms that are a part of them. With the right structures for gathering and sharing the wisdom of the network, they can be "smarter" than any individual member. This means that a strong network is more than the collection of a set of strong players: It also depends on how the

> *Networks can work "smarter" than the individuals or firms that are a part of them. Orchestration is what makes smart networks smart.*

members of the network are organized and how they interact.

"Flat world" technologies have the potential to draw groups of people or firms together for a common goal, whether it is connecting with friends or tapping into global innovation networks to find the next hit product. Groups of people working together in systems that are well orchestrated can develop projects that are beyond the scope of their individual capacities. Howard Rheingold's *Smart Mobs: The Next Social Revolution* explores how wireless technologies are linking people together in temporary networks or "ad-hocracies."[21] In *Wikinomics: How Mass Collaboration Changes Everything*, Don Tapscott and Anthony Williams examine how companies are using networks to work together to solve problems and create value.[22] Recognition of the power of the network is increasing.

Online communities are demonstrating some of the possibilities for tapping into the wisdom of the network. Computer software makers increasingly rely upon a network of users (particularly if they have a dedicated user base) to respond to customer questions, reducing the need for customer support, and to test software, reducing the need for internal testing. Companies are using internal betting markets to make sales forecasts and public auctions to underwrite insurance policies.

Building on the Wikipedia model, the "We Are Smarter Than Me" project was launched in 2006 to test whether a book could be written (and ultimately published) by tapping into the collective wisdom of the community. The project, sponsored by Pearson, Wharton School Publishing, The Wharton School's SEI Center for Advanced Studies in Management, and MIT's Center for Collective Intelligence and Shared Insights, invited more than a million participants to write and edit the online book. It is testing the limits of community collaboration to produce an intellectual and commercial product.

Another group is even designing an open-source automobile. Markus Merz, a former BMW employee, started the Open-Source Car project (or OScar), which has brought together more than a thousand participants to create a four-door electric vehicle.[23] The community exchanges ideas in forums moderated by volunteers, and the best ideas are incorporated into the car design. The project has yet to produce a prototype (let alone engage in crash tests and other trials), but it does show that open-source models are beginning to migrate from software and knowledge to the creation of physical products.

But crowds are not always smart. Remember Surowiecki says that they are smart "under the right circumstances." Under the wrong conditions, crowds can often have less wisdom than individuals. Many examples point to how "groupthink" has led crowds of people over the edge like a pack of lemmings. The group tends to reinforce the current mental model, and this filters out great ideas and the perspective of outliers. So it is not enough to just bring together a great group of smart minds; there need to be the right circumstances. One of the right circumstances is having someone looking across the network, organizing it, creating frameworks and platforms, and drawing together the right people. This is the network orchestrator.

Smarter networks do not just happen. They require guidance, intelligence, a design, and an invisible or visible hand drawing together all the diverse contributions. In other words, they require orchestration. Otherwise, crowds can rapidly devolve into chaos and stupidity. Orchestration is what makes smart networks smart.

Beyond the Cheapest Needle: The Logic of the Network

A fixed supply chain or service value chain is built to deliver a specific product or service. The supply chain manager must access the specific capabilities needed for that goal. A broader network, on the other hand, must be designed to offer the broader capabilities that are useful now and might be useful in the future. What are these capabilities? What is the logic of network design?

Whereas quotas or cost savings were once the primary drivers in the decision to shift manufacturing abroad—and still play a major role in such decisions—companies are increasingly recognizing other factors as well. The lowest-cost location might not always win. In outsourcing serv-ices, cost is also not always the primary reason to look abroad. A Bureau of National Affairs survey of human resources outsourcing in 2004 found that the top two reasons for outsourcing were gaining access to greater expertise and improving service quality. Only 28 percent of respondents cited cost-cutting as a primary driver.[24] Beyond price, the logic of global networks might be based on accessing best-in-world capabilities, increasing resilience, boosting speed, capitalizing on col-laboration, navigating global trade restrictions, and establishing stan-dards. In designing the best net-works, we need to look at each of these benefits of the network, as explored in more detail on the fol-lowing pages.

> *Although quotas or cost savings were once the primary drivers in the decision to shift manufac-turing abroad, companies are increasingly recogniz-ing other factors, such as accessing best-in-world capabilities, increasing resilience, boosting speed, capitalizing on collabora-tion, navigating global trade restrictions, and establishing standards.*

Feed Me More Mommy! Accessing Best-in-Class Capabilities

Networks need to be designed to offer access to diverse capabilities. The Baby Talk doll can tell us a lot about the potential of dispersed manufacturing, despite her fairly limited vocabulary. When the Baby Talk doll was introduced in the 1980s, it represented a revolution in toy making (see Figure 3-1). This blonde haired, blue-eyed marvel was described as an "animated talk-a-tronic" toy. It required a new word to describe how it was different from the old pull-string talking dolls. When a child finished giving the doll a bottle, the baby would respond by saying "Mmmmm, that was good." Pull out the bottle too soon, and the baby would demand "Feed me more, Mommy!" Pick up the doll, and it would say, "I love to be picked up." It was almost human. Although these words were not as profound at Neil Arm-strong's "one small step for man, one giant leap for mankind," they represented a profound breakthrough in drawing together diverse capabilities through dispersed manufacturing.

FIGURE 3-1   Baby Talk doll

Dispersed manufacturing allows for the development of products such as Baby Talk that are fundamentally different. It does this by bringing together the best components from different parts of the world. The Baby Talk doll used the best computer chips from Taiwan, the best vinyl body assembled in mainland China, and the best fabrics from Korea. Borderless manufacturing brought all these together—the best components from the best sources—into a single doll.

The network needs to seek out best-in-the-world capabilities, wherever they are in the world. In making porcelain dinnerware, for example, the best decals for the decoration come from Japan, and because they are relatively inexpensive and easy to ship, they can be sent to China, where the best and cheapest porcelain work is done. The result is outstanding quality for the decals as well as the dinner set, at a reasonable price. This is better than what could have been done in either Japan or China alone.

In some cases, certain parts of the world are centers for specific capabilities. For example, certain types of casual cotton shirts are best made in India, but finer white cotton dress shirts might come from China or Korea. Certain types and styles of fancy embroidering or beadwork are centered in certain cities or regions, and it makes sense to go to these regions for this work. As John Hagel and John Seely Brown point out in *The Only Sustainable Edge,* the real power of outsourcing is in accessing capabilities. Companies can use outsourcing to accelerate capability building by accessing the best capabilities in the world.[25]

9/11 and SARS: Building Resilience

Networks also have to be designed to increase flexibility and resilience. Shocks are a fact of life in the modern world. These shocks can come from regulatory changes but also from economic, political, and natural catastrophes. The impact of these disruptions was graphically demonstrated by the 9/11 terrorist attacks in the United States and the SARS outbreak in Asia.

Following the terrorist attacks on New York and Washington, D.C., on September 11, 2001, many retailers thought the American consumer economy would come to a crashing halt. When one panicked retailer called Hong Kong to cancel a line of high-fashion parachute pants, Li & Fung proposed changing the order to one for basic, all-season pants and reserving the zippers for other products. In the end, consumers kept buying and the retailer renewed its order for parachute pants. Li & Fung was also able to quickly shift production from high-risk countries to low-risk ones, reallocating hundreds of millions of dollars' worth of merchandise in just a week's time.

With the outbreak of severe acute respiratory syndrome (SARS) in Hong Kong in March 2003, the World Health Organization issued a warning in early April against travel to Hong Kong and South China. Some of Li & Fung's overseas customers canceled their trips to the Chinese mainland for the subsequent two months, which is a busy procurement season. In response to customers' requests, the company allocated manufacturing orders among several mainland factories, in case any of them had to be shut down because of SARS. In view of possible loss of business, Li & Fung arranged to conduct videoconferences with customers and moved half of its top management team to the U.S. and European offices. The company lost only about 5 percent of orders in this period that devastated other companies in the region. Like the Internet, this network of suppliers is a resilient system that is built to survive catastrophe.

This process of midcourse corrections happens on a smaller scale all the time. As exchange rates fluctuate, demand changes, or regulations shift, the network orchestrator can change the supply chain in response. An orchestrator, such as Li & Fung, can broker multiple deals on all levels simultaneously, sending raw materials to manufacturers, linking factories with each other, managing logistics and distribution networks, and building knowledge networks around customers to support product design and development. The company can easily divert orders from countries or regions beset by economic or political crises to others that are more stable because it has a network that is broad and diverse.

Some resilient systems are designed to have redundancy, such as backup telephone networks or information systems, but a dispersed network has many more degrees of freedom. Instead of merely backing up a given capability, the system can be dynamically reconfigured to move various processes to different locations around the world. Instead of one or two backup facilities, thousands of factories can be brought together into new supply chains.

Two Million Christmas Trees: Boosting Speed

Networks also have to be designed to increase speed. Even in a flat world, Christmas comes only once a year. The gifts and wrapping paper that are so highly valued on December 24 are marked down by 50 percent or more on December 26. So when Coca-Cola in Mexico needed a rush order to manufacture a unique Coca-Cola Christmas tree as a premium, the deadline was not negotiable.

The tree was a small wonder, a green polystyrene tree about a foot high, with a toy train running around its base, flashing colored LED lights in its branches and decorations emblazoned with Coca-Cola bottles, Santas, and polar bears. A small white light in the interior rotated as the tree played Christmas music. The light shone through the ornaments to project dancing stars, Coke bottles, and other images on the walls. Practically speaking, however, all these features made it an extremely complicated product to produce. It required pulling together many capabilities from diverse suppliers.

Molded out of plastic, the tree demanded 40 to 50 tools and hundreds of molds. And Coca-Cola needed two million of these trees before the holiday season.

This project might typically take a year or more to complete. It was finished in four and a half months. To compress the manufacturing time, Li & Fung used three factories simultaneously to manufacture the trees. The factories chosen to fulfill this order were located near one another, to facilitate sharing component parts. The IC chips came from Taiwan, where the best-in-class chip-making companies are located. When the chips ran short, the company sent an employee down by airplane to bring back more; it could not afford a lull in the action. The cost of the $200 airline ticket to retrieve the tiny chips was small in comparison to the cost of shutting down the line or paying to air-freight the final product.

While running production in parallel, Li & Fung closely monitored each of the factories to ensure that products from all factories looked the same. It took only ten weeks to finish all steps, from design to product delivery. By October, 700 containers of Christmas trees were shipped to Coca-Cola. The promotion was a huge success. Now every year that promotion and other work from Coca-Cola has come to Li & Fung—but the sourcing of the projects is usually from a different set of suppliers each time.

Dispersed manufacturing can reduce cycle time. Historically, it took 12 to 15 months to develop a line of clothing and deliver it to retailers. So for the line expected in spring 2008, work would begin in the summer of 2006. Now production can be compressed to as little as 45 days, although typically six or seven months are involved in designing and sampling to refine the concept and show it to retailers. Reorders can be done in as little as 15 days.

A broad network allows for parallel processing that accelerates the change. Another strategy for increasing speed is to design a network that allows for initial production to be carried out in the most cost-effective market and for reorders to be made in another country close to the end market. For example, for the U.S. retail market, initial production could be in China to lower cost, but if the product sells well, reorders for quick delivery can be made in Central America, shaving weeks off the trip to market. The Chinese fabric can be shipped there waiting to be cut. When the reorder comes in, it can quickly be finished and shipped north to catch the season, albeit at a higher cost. But this would be sales that would otherwise be lost.

Networks have to be broad enough and have enough capacity to allow the production to be completed quickly through parallel paths, when needed. Networks also have to be matched to the needs of customers. Some do not need such a quick response time, so the network must include slower, lower-cost suppliers that can produce good-quality products more slowly and cheaply. But companies that require quick response—to meet the demands of rapid fashion changes, for example—can achieve faster turnaround by moving production to different locations.

Improving Forecasts: Increasing Responsiveness

Orchestrating the entire supply chain also allows companies to delay ordering and sourcing decisions, which can improve forecasting and reduce costs of markdowns or stockouts at retail. In a world of short product cycles, forecasting demand is a challenge. Even if forecasts are accurate when they are made, in a flat world where consumers' tastes are changing rapidly, the forecast could be wrong by the time the product arrives. Faster production and delivery can allow for delayed forecasting and delayed ordering decisions, so the big bets can be made as late in the process as possible. For products that do not have rapid fashion changes—basic polo shirts or sheets and towels, for example—it is possible for the retailer to hold a good buffer in reserve to meet any fluctuations, but this also increases warehousing costs. So even here, the capacity to manufacture and deliver products as quickly as possible is still very important.

Flexible commitments can lock up the capacity of a supplier without specifying the final design and color until the last moment. The trust between Li & Fung and its supplier network means that it can reserve undyed yarn from the yarn supplier. This locks up capacity at the mills for the weaving and dyeing, with the promise that they will get an order of a specified size, but no details. Five weeks before delivery, Li & Fung lets the supplier know which colors to use and when additional fabric and trim will be delivered. The factory then has three weeks to deliver the final garments. This orchestration gives suppliers predictability, while providing buyers with rapid and accurate response.

Under the old import model, this would not have been possible. Thousands of miles away, the manufacturer was a black box. Customers would send orders to factories with specifications in advance. They needed the complete order to ensure that the factory could produce it in time. By orchestrating the entire chain, Li & Fung opened the black box, making it possible to wait until the last minute to make decisions. If purple is no longer selling, the orchestrator can dye the wool another color. If a certain weave has become popular, it can shift its processes. When the fabric is on the cutting table and long sleeves are no longer selling, it can ask the factory to cut them short. By opening the black box, Li & Fung creates the opportunity to adapt *even after the initial buyer order.*

Floral Buttons: Discovering New Resources

The orchestrator always needs to be on the lookout for new capabilities that answer questions that customers have not even asked. For example, the lead designer of a new garment in New York might specify a line of clothing with a floral pattern, but a designer close to the factory in India might know of a new button that has been produced with a floral pattern that the designers in New York have not seen. This fits perfectly with the new design. The on-site designer might also suggest a modification that will make the product easier, cheaper, or faster to produce. Communications links around the world create opportunities to share knowledge and engage remote partners in collaborating on new designs. The network needs to have enough diversity to bring these new insights to the table and to share them with partners wherever they are in the world.

Maintaining Continuity of Supply for South Africa: Navigating Shifting Global Trade Regulations

Markets can change overnight. For example, on a Friday in early September 2006, the South African government announced that it would be imposing strict quotas on Chinese imports in two weeks. Li &

Fung had orders already in production for South African retailers that would be affected by these changes. Managers began to look at contingency plans to move production to factories in different countries and even to move the last stage of existing orders to different end countries to satisfy non-China country-of-origin rules. The network needs to be broad enough, global enough, and flexible enough to meet such shifts in national or global trade.

The lumps and bumps of the flat world make orchestration all the more important. In addition to managing networks, designing and empowering supply chains, and deriving value from the broader network, the orchestrator can adjust supply chains and networks to the current terrain of the world.

RFID: Creating Standards

Radio Frequency Identification (RFID) tags contain an integrated circuit that is so small that it can be hidden under a sticker as small as a postage stamp, for product identification, or under the skin of a patient, for medical identification. Powered by the radio waves of the reader, the RFID tag sends back data to the reader wirelessly. This replaces clumsier bar codes for product identification, making it possible to more easily monitor the movement of a box full of products or even individual products throughout the supply chain. The tags are also used in passports, transit passes, libraries, and animal identification. The lowest-cost tags, such as the EPC RFID chosen as the standard by the U.S. Department of Defense, Wal-Mart, and other major retailers, sell for a few cents each.

The network can play a powerful role in establishing standards for such new technology, as demonstrated by the rise of the GSM standard in European wireless, now accounting for more than 80 percent of mobile systems worldwide, in contrast to the mix of standards that emerged in the United States. A powerful player in a supply network such as Wal-Mart can be instrumental in establishing such standards. Wal-Mart required its top 100 suppliers to use RFID tags for all shipments starting in January 2005, to improve supply chain management.

Clear standards often benefit all the players in a network, as the Win-Tel standard (Microsoft Windows operating system and Intel chips) in personal computing demonstrated. The standard helped the partners in the network compete against rivals such as Apple, which, by holding its proprietary computer technology tightly, limited its growth in personal computing. Standards, which are particularly important in technology-based businesses, can help organize a network and often allow one network to compete more effectively against another. The victory of Matsushita's VHS technology in video over Sony's Betamax, which was considered technologically superior, was largely attributed to the ability of Matsushita to draw together a network of content providers, equipment manufacturers, and other companies to adopt the standard. The network orchestrator can play an important role in establishing and implementing standards that benefit the entire network.

Clustering in a Flat World

Although the flat world has made clustering less important, many clusters remain. In a flat world, the challenge is to balance the benefits of being part of a single cluster with the benefits of being part of multiple sets of clusters. Some regions of the world still have specialized skills—many of them, in fact. Not all the films in the world are made in Hollywood. Clusters of expertise exist in Bollywood in India, Hong Kong, and other regions. And even Hollywood filmmakers turn to different parts of the world to lower costs and access expertise in animation, martial arts, or other skills. Silicon Valley is still a substantial center for emerging technologies, but there are many other centers now around the globe in places such as Boston, Bangalore, and Tel Aviv. The best porcelain in the world comes from China, the

> *Although the flat world has made clustering less important, many clusters remain or can even become stronger. In a flat world, the challenge is to balance the benefits of being part of a single cluster with the benefits of being part of multiple clusters.*

best leather comes from Korea, and the highest-quality and cheapest-cost sewing comes from Vietnam and Bangladesh.

Some of these skills take time to develop, as does the creation of a critical mass of supporting resources (from universities to venture capital). This means that despite continued decline in logistics and communications costs, there may be compelling reasons for clusters to continue to exist. In addition, clusters and colocation are more important when a lot of human interaction is needed for innovation and creativity, such as for R&D. Network orchestrators need to be aware of these clusters and tap into them.

These new clusters can be across countries and within countries. Within the Yangtze River Delta region of China, the city of Taizhou is known for auto parts, handicrafts and arts, and rubber products; Shanghai is home to clusters of companies in areas such as refined steel, petroleum, and chemicals. In designing networks, orchestrators need to recognize these clusters and identify suppliers in regions that offer capabilities needed by the network.

Because products are physical, geography is still important, but not as important as it used to be. About 40 percent of Li & Fung's orders are sourced from China, so its location in Hong Kong and knowledge of local language, culture, and policy is beneficial. But the flexibility of geography can be seen in the company's sourcing from 40 different countries. Geography is not irrelevant, as it is with digital goods, but it is becoming less important. The additional costs of moving the stages of production to different countries need to be weighed against many other factors, including quality, cost, time, regulations, and the location of the customer. Rapid reduction in costs of logistics, coordination, and communication mean that it is more important to find the *best* location for each stage in the process instead of the *closest*.

Li & Fung's networks are designed to produce physical goods. When networks are engaged in creating digital rather than physical outputs, virtual clusters emerge. User groups and online communities come together to collaborate. Linux developers and the Wikipedia community can be anywhere in the world, but they are drawn together by common interests and a shared project. Even in these networks, certain nodes emerge as more important than others, with more connections within the network or to other networks.

These nodes emerge as the new hubs of a set of clusters that are not limited by geography.

In a flat world, the challenge is to balance the benefits of being part of a single cluster with the benefits of being part of multiple clusters. Companies might be part of geographic clusters that are linked to global clusters around common interests or expertise, as well as clusters based on delivering a specific type of product or service. A single company might thus be involved in several different clusters at the same time.

A Robust Network

A robust network is the soil from which customer solutions spring. Creating a robust network requires anticipating the capabilities that might be needed in the future and assessing what might need to be done and where. This demands that orchestrators have their ears to the ground to anticipate how the world is changing. Greater "peripheral vision" is needed to sense weak signals and respond to them.[26] The network itself can offer outposts for sensing changes in the world and responding to them.

> *A robust network is the soil from which customer solutions spring.*

Listening to the feedback of the network is therefore crucial to success. Orchestrators also need to monitor the environment to anticipate changes. The orchestrator needs to augment or reshape the network to respond to these changes. In a flat world, the strength of a business is not based on the assets and capabilities that it owns; these can sometimes be a weakness if they are made obsolete by changes in the environment. Most important are the assets and capabilities that the business is connected to. The richer and deeper this network of connections is, the better the orchestrator will be able to draw forth the right solution when a customer demand arises.

Trust and Relationships

What binds the network together? Information technology, of course, is essential. Complex and fluid networks and organizations require advanced information technology and management science tools for configuring the network, valuing options, identifying profit opportunities, and managing risk. Technology and advanced modeling have made these tools more powerful. Information technology is at the center of the flattening of the world. It keeps all the members of the orchestra on the same page at the same time. It allows them to move forward in concert, regardless of where they are in the world. Although information technology has transformed business organizations, the heart of any network and enterprise consists of human judgment, trust, human relationships, and business processes.

In building dispersed supply chains, many things can and do go wrong. This is where trust and relationships are essential. A few phone calls can resolve situations that could be tied up in debate and litigation for months or years. Although the network is dispersed and the supply chain is temporary, thick connections of

> *Although information technology is at the center of flattening the world, the heart of any network and enterprise consists of human judgment, trust, human relationships, and business processes.*

both personal relationships and technology are the glue that binds this loose network and makes it work. The network orchestrator builds and nurtures these relationships.

These relationships help to work out the inevitable smaller bumps along the way. For example, a new buyer for a customer had been in discussions about a new sheet-and-towel program but had neglected to mention the advertisement date and in-store date. In early September, the buyer said it needed the product in stores by the end of November. A Li & Fung executive picked up the phone to call suppliers to see what they could do. Then he called the CEO of the retailer, apologized for the miscommunication, and found out exactly how much product was needed in stores on November 30. The first shipment was by air, with the cost split between Li & Fung and the retailer. The rest could come later by water, to reduce costs. These types of bumps in the road come up every day; personal connections help to resolve them.

The need for trust in networks may explain the persistence of the physical interactions in an online world. Even one of the most popular political blogging sites had its first face-to-face meeting in Las Vegas in 2006, which brought out politicians to press the flesh of these once-disembodied bloggers. This is somewhat surprising if you consider that blogs are designed for some level of anonymity and placeless interaction. The technology does not require physical interaction; the humans in the system do. At some point, even a purely electronic community leads to a desire for physical interaction. This is a powerful commentary on the limits of the technology.

One might imagine that, in a flat, digitally connected world, machines would resolve problems and overall design of optimal networks and supply chains. But smoothing these bumps and dealing with the complexity of modern networks depends more than ever on old-fashioned trust and personal relationships.

A Machete and a PDA

In building and managing networks, orchestrators need to work in a flat world and an unflat world at the same time. The image of the traditional trader is a khaki-clad adventurer with a machete in hand slicing his way through the jungles to find the best suppliers and products. The modern Li & Fung trader is more likely to carry a cell phone and a PDA (symbols of the flat world—borderless and always connected) as well as a machete. This trader must cut through the underbrush to locate the next most cost-competitive factory, while at the same time bridging the IT gap by downloading point-of-sale information on the smart phone from retailers in sophisticated developed markets. The Li & Fung trader might be sending text messages to a buyer in New York even while wielding the machete on the ground.

The jungles have not gone away with the flat world. The mountains are still just as high. The day-to-day challenges of turning raw materials into finished goods have not been diminished—just transformed. The yarn still needs to be woven into a certain pattern. The stitches still need to be even and tight, the buttons secure, and the color fast. This is the reality of competing in a flat world. Success requires both the machete and the PDA—and the presence to know which one to lift up to your ear when the phone rings.

Are You Ready for the Flat World?

- How do your supply chains compete against those of others? Which supply chains in your industry are winning? Losing? Why?

- Where are the opportunities to move to more cooperative relationships?

- How broad is your network from which your supply chain is drawn?

- What are the capabilities of your network? What capabilities will you need in the future?

- How can your networks be strengthened?

- How are you building trust and relationships, as well as technological connections?

- Given the need to compete network against network, what do you need to do next?

Part II

Management: Control and Empowerment

Companies need to balance managing through internal controls with empowering employees, customers, and suppliers across more flexible networks.

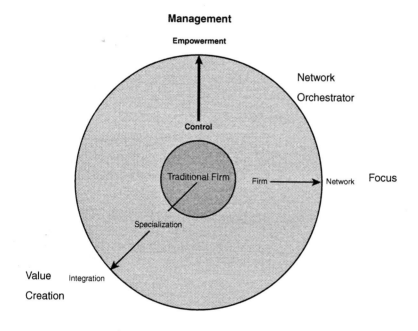

4

Take Responsibility for the Whole Chain (Whether You Own It or Not)

How can companies take responsibility for factories that they do not own, particularly in a world in which human rights, environmental impact, and other areas of social responsibility are attracting more intense scrutiny? The answer is focusing on taking responsibility for the whole network and using rigorous compliance auditing, prevention, inspection, training, and other levers to achieve this goal.

About 70 minutes by high-speed ferry up the coast of China from Hong Kong, the city of Zhuhai has become a major manufacturing center. The Mun Li Garment Factory was started there by Jimmy Leung 15 years ago after the success of his first factory in Macau. His Zhuhai factory now has 1,000 workers in peak times and is a key supplier to Li & Fung's clients and other top-tier U.S. and European brands.

With its success, Mun Li recently built a striking new factory and office building in Zhuhai. The new building was designed in consultation with a master of Feng Shui, an ancient Chinese art of design for improving the flow of energy, or *chi*. A waterfall flows through a central atrium outside the conference room where buyers come a few times a week during the fall to discuss their spring lines. The water cascades down to a fish pond in the middle of the front drive, where orange and white carp dash among the lily pads. It is an arrangement that is designed to gather wealth like the water in the pool. So far, it seems to be working, although it is uncertain whether it is a result of the good chi of the fish pond or the bigger economic and political forces that have built a booming Chinese garment industry.

The factory's success also depends on rigorous inspection at every stage of the process and the ability to meet stringent working condition required by of customers. Rolls of fabric are everywhere, and inspectors examine about 40 percent of the rolls inch by inch for defects that are flagged. If they find too many defects, they return the cloth. The factory performs inspections after each stage of the production process—cutting, sewing, washing and ironing. The treatment of workers in the factory is of intense interest to consumers in developed countries and the retailers who serve them. These customers want to know that no children are working in the factory and that when the bell rings at noon, as it does, the sewing machines shut down and the workers pour out into the stairwell for lunch. Buyers want to know that the factory has enough bathrooms and that other conditions are good. With rising attention to global warming and pollution, they also are increasingly concerned about environmental impact. They expect manufacturers to follow proper compliance standards. So the retailers who order this clothing need to keep close tabs on factories on the other side of the world that they do not even own.

> *With rising demands for corporate social responsibility, retailers and network orchestrators need to keep close tabs on factories on the other side of the world that they do not even own.*

This is one of the fundamental challenges of dispersed manufacturing. To be competitive and enhance flexibility, companies need to use networks and dispersed manufacturing. But who is minding the factory when the factory might change with every order?

There Is Greater Transparency in a Flat World

In a flat world characterized by the free flow of information and consumer-generated content, if a violation occurs anywhere in the world, consumers and the media might know about it everywhere, often before the companies themselves. This was a lesson that companies from Nike to Wal-Mart, to McDonald's found out the hard way in the early days of offshoring. In 2000, activists with the Hong Kong Christian Industrial Committee (HKCIC) reported that toys for McDonald's Happy Meals were being produced by a supplier that employed children as young as 14 years old. The children said they had lied about their age to obtain the jobs. According to reports in the *Sunday Morning Post of Hong Kong*, they were working 16-hour days for less than $3 per day, earning less than the cost of a Happy Meal.

> *In a flat world, if a violation occurs anywhere in the world, consumers and the media might know about it everywhere, often before the companies themselves.*

McDonald's had outsourced the production of its Happy Meal toys to Simon Marketing Hong Kong, Ltd. That company, in turn, hired a factory in Hong Kong—City Toys, Ltd.—to make the toys. The company employed about 2,000 workers, and these workers were the focus of the allegations. When the story broke, the factory and McDonald's said they had not found evidence to support the claims, but it did not matter. It also did not matter that McDonald's was not the owner of the factory. The damage had been done. All the consumers and critics saw were McDonald's toys being made by underage workers. The Child Labour News Service, for example, ran headlines reading "Little Slaves Pack (Un)Happy Meals."[27]

Consumers and activists did not focus on Simon or City Toys. They held McDonald's responsible for the whole chain. The company with the brand on the label, or a retailer who is responsible to the company with the brand on the label, has to answer for every step of the manufacturing process. In a world of increasing transparency and advocacy, there are no secrets, even in the remotest corner of the remotest factory in Asia.

Consumers and investors are paying attention to this information. A survey of more than 21,000 customers by the Reputation Institute suggests that "almost unanimously, the public says it wants information about a company's record on social and environmental responsibility to help decide which companies to buy from, invest in, and work for."[28] Ethically active consumers, estimated to account for 12 to 20 percent of consumer markets in developed countries, tend to punish companies for corporate social responsibility (CSR) lapses, as reflected in reduced sales, lower stock price, and higher staff turnover. In the United States, Germany, Australia, and Canada, one in five investors claims to read company corporate social and environmental reports when making investment decisions. And this is only going to rise.

Consumers once were more concerned about getting good quality at a low price than where their products came from. Today they care about both the product *and* the process by which it is made. They want good prices, good quality—and the assurance that workers are well treated and the environment is protected. Customers are making new demands, not only for quality and flexibility, but also for transparency of the manufacturing supply chain.

Whereas missteps in social responsibility can be costly, socially responsible action can pay off for companies by leading to greater customer loyalty and increased revenues. In a flat world, there are no hidden corners of the world. The free flow of information that has permitted network orchestration has also created a world in which companies need to be conscious of the actions of their entire network, even if they do not own it.

Minding the Factory

It might seem that the best way to ensure factories' rigorous compliance with social and environmental objectives would be to keep all the stages of the manufacturing process in a single, wholly owned factory. But this would mean sacrificing the flexibility and other advantages of dispersed manufacturing. This has led Li & Fung and other network orchestrators to a different model. The suppliers remain independent, but control is achieved through education, rigorous monitoring, and testing to ensure compliance. The supply chain is loosely linked, but compliance systems are tight.

> *The supply chain is loosely linked, but compliance systems are tight.*

Back at the factory in Zhuhai, at the far end of a sewing line on the second floor, where 250 workers are busy piecing together the cut material that will become sweatshirts or women's dress blouses, is a room that belongs to Li & Fung. A Li & Fung inspector looks over a set of red-and-black fleece jackets bearing $68 price tags for the U.S. market. Because the jackets are for the current season, they are being sent by more expensive air freight. They should be out the door, through the U.S. distribution center and in stores within a week.

The Li & Fung inspector at the Zhuhai plant is there every day, keeping a constant eye on projects to make sure that schedules are on track and that the final product will be acceptable to the end retailer. In addition to inspecting products, the company has to monitor working conditions and send compliance inspectors to make sure work rules are followed and workers are treated well. Clients also have their own third-party inspectors who make surprise visits to ensure compliance. Customers in the U.S. and other parts of the world hold the treatment of workers as a key concern. The factory, Li & Fung, and end customers all sharply watch for compliance.

Addressing the Root Cause: Control Without Ownership

Allan Wong's office at Li & Fung is like a small museum, with an ancient hand-powered sewing machine, spindles, an antique iron, and a wooden tabletop hand-loom. A self-described "garment man," he has deep roots in the industry. But the world he works in has become far more complex. He now faces the challenge of ensuring the standards and compliance of partners in factories that the company does not own.

Understanding and ensuring compliance requires understanding not only global standards and local law, but also the manufacturing process and industry itself. Compliance issues are not at all abstract.

They relate to how manufacturing processes are organized and basic issues such as work policies. The solutions also have to be created to achieve customer goals while allowing factory owners to make a profit. The right solutions often can achieve both goals because better operating processes and technologies can create more productive operations while improving working conditions. "When you want to address a problem, you have to address the root cause," Wong says. "You have to identify what is the problem and determine how to address the problem."

> *Compliance in this world is much more about carrots than sticks (although there is combination of both). The focus is primarily on setting clear guidelines, offering education, and then inspecting to ensure results.*

Compliance in this world is much more about carrots than sticks (although there is a combination of both). The focus is primarily on setting clear guidelines, offering education, and then inspecting to ensure results.

Creating a Code of Conduct

Creating a code of conduct and business processes can help ensure compliance even in a world of dispersed manufacturing. Where rigid control of day-to-day operations might not be possible, or even desirable, a set of "laws" and policy manuals that govern the actions of all members in the supply chain can be a powerful way to ensure that all players understand what is expected of the entire network.

Li & Fung, for example, has developed a thick manual of "Labor Standards and Relevant Local Law Guidelines" for 20 different countries. The company shares this information at no cost with associates, factories, and customers. The manual specifies details of operations down to the type of fire extinguishers and the contents of the first aid box. There are standards for the treatment of workers, minimum wages, health and environmental protection, water quality, noise pollution, and lighting. This ensures that everyone is literally on the same page. The code is a set of rigorous labor, health, and environmental standards based on national labor laws; International Labor

Organization (ILO) conventions and treaties; and international best practices. For example, suppliers are prohibited from hiring child or involuntary labor and from practicing corporal punishment or any form of discrimination. The code also highlights the importance of environmental protection. It shows factories how to do their work without dictating what to do.

The standards also call for mandatory or voluntary measures to reduce environmental impact. Li & Fung suppliers are monitored for the reduction of waste from electrical and electronic equipment (to comply with European directives) and restricted hazardous substances. Monitoring verifies the treatment and disposal of wastewater effluents at vendor factories. In addition, voluntary measures encourage vendors to responsibly source timber, use organic cotton, and improve clean air to meet the Guangdong Pearl River Clean Air Charter.

Beyond the minimum standard of expectations, certain customers have specific demands for CSR or other issues, just as they might have demands for production quality, speed, or the use of materials. To serve these customers, vendors need to comply with specific customer standards for human rights or in areas such as recycling, minimizing of packaging waste, and sustainable development. Not every supplier will be a good fit for meeting all these expectations. Understanding the capabilities of suppliers and carefully matching customers to suppliers can help fulfill all the customer's requirements.

Education is critical so that suppliers understand what needs to be done and how to achieve it. Li & Fung is active in promotion, education, and training on social responsibility and labor rights. Wong himself has facilitated more than 120 training seminars in 20 countries on compliance. Companies can take a total quality management approach to improving processes and outcomes. The focus is not on catching problems but on confirming good work. Because orchestrators work with many different suppliers and customers, they play a vital role in sharing best practices across the network through codes of conduct and training programs.

Monitoring Rigorously

Creating a code is not enough. Rigorous monitoring and certification are also needed. Factory conditions can change over time, and customer expectations can shift. An annual recertification process ensures that companies are actively tested for their ability to meet expectations, rather than waiting for problems to emerge and correcting them after the fact. This helps ensure ongoing and active compliance, and eliminates any tendency to ignore problems.

Every standard must be measurable so that factories and inspectors can determine whether the company is in compliance. Li & Fung's process includes a preliminary audit, corrective action plans for those that fall short in some area, a final audit, and periodic unannounced audits. Every new vendor is audited this way, and existing vendors are renewed annually before the end of May. The same set of rules applies to the contractors that the vendors might hire to fulfill the order.

This monitoring covers compliance by physically inspecting factories, interviewing management to understand the factory culture and practices; reviewing workers' wages, working hours, age, health, safety, and other records for reliability and completeness; and interviewing workers to ascertain that factory policies and practices are in compliance. For each new supplier, the local compliance officer conducts a comprehensive inspection before signing the contract. Suppliers are required to fill out a Factory Profile form that includes the operation details and working conditions inside the factory.

After inspection, compliance auditors submit the evaluation results to the supplier and provide recommendations for making necessary changes. In some cases, the compliance auditors revisit the supplier several times to make sure the procedures are followed. Each supplier is closely monitored throughout the year, and an annual audit check ensures that suppliers continue to comply with the Code. Conscious or repeated violation of the Code results in the cancellation of orders or loss of status as an approved supplier to Li & Fung.

Anticipating

The system also focuses on anticipating and preventing potential problems. Where are the weak points? What could go wrong? Small problems indicate weaknesses that need to be addressed. The company can assess these trouble spots and then move quickly to remedy them. Companies in chemicals, nuclear power, and other high-risk industries have created formal mechanisms to identify and analyze their "near misses," which are often given little attention because they did not have disastrous consequence.

To better prevent problems, orchestrators also have to pay attention to emerging consumer trends. The rise of concern about human rights was clear long before it became a topic of widespread concern and activism. Similarly, concerns about the environment are growing, even though the formal regulations and actions in this area have still not fully hit the manufacturing industry. It pays to recognize where the world is headed and get out in front. It is much easier to prevent a problem when it is small than to try to rebuild after a full-blown disaster.

Post-mortems are critical in learning from problems. The Mayo Clinic and other medical institutions learn from experience by conducting post-mortems on their cases. Doctors assemble as a team once a week to discuss any complications or negative outcomes during the week. Military leaders conduct "after-action reviews" to improve strategies and tactics. Professional football players watch videos of their past games to improve their play. This increases the opportunity to learn from the past, and reduces risks of repeating mistakes in the future. By conducting such post-mortems, the orchestrator can ensure that the network continues to learn and improve.

Ensuring Accountability

Although the focus is on the carrot, the stick is also involved. Suppliers who fall short are cut off. A supplier that is not in compliance cannot be contracted or paid through Li & Fung's systems, which block the merchandising teams from placing an order. The factories must be compliant in three primary areas: country of origin, labor standards, and supply chain security. After the order has been fulfilled, if the full set of documents for country of origin compliance is not on file, the vendor cannot be paid. Li & Fung has zero tolerance. If a problem is identified in the middle of filling the order, production is stopped. Although some suppliers are shut out in the process, the primary focus is on helping suppliers meet expectations while respecting their independence.

Keeping the monitoring division independent from the business units is important. Decisions about compliance should not be colored or influenced by business imperatives. Otherwise, managers might have an incentive to cut corners on compliance to improve the returns of their business. The organization must recognize the significance of compliance issues for the company's reputation and long-term success.

The compliance function also needs "teeth." Its focus might be to work with suppliers to help them come into compliance, but the compliance office needs enforcement power. This is the true test of the system. Companies with excellent corporate values on paper have gotten into trouble because company leaders did not act on those principles. The compliance office needs the ability and resources to act autonomously and swiftly to address problems, even at the expense of short-term earnings.

Creating the Context

In addition to their individual initiatives, groups of companies are collaborating more broadly to improve working conditions and address environmental concerns. Business for Social Responsibility (BSR), for example, is an organization that promotes the respect for ethical values, people, the community, and the environment. For example, in conjunction with a BSR labor rights project in 2002, Li & Fung, together with several other U.S.-branded companies, created a "labor rights pocket guide" along with a labor law protection and aid poster specifically targeted toward migrant factory workers of Guangdong, China.

Companies also are collaborating with the United Nation's Global Compact, which has created a platform to promote human rights, labor welfare, and the environment through good practices. The Dow Jones Sustainability World Indexes track the performance of companies worldwide that lead their industry in corporate sustainability: social, economic, and environmental responsibilities. Participating in such broader initiatives helps to define and level the playing field for everyone.

Extending the Supply Chain: Return, Recycle, Reuse

The supply chain used to end with the delivery of the product to the retailer or customer. But in an age of growing concern about environmental impact, companies have to take responsibility for more of the chain, from R&D through manufacturing, marketing, distribution, and even recycling and reuse. Hewlett-Packard has created systems to return and reuse spent print cartridges, Ikea is recycling wood chips and other materials, and flooring maker Shaw Industries is turning trash carpet into new materials. Shaw's Used Carpet Reclamation Project, one of its many environmental initiatives, is collecting almost 90 million pounds of post-consumer carpet waste and 10 million pounds of industrial carpet waste every year to supply its Evergreen Nylon Recycling Facility in Augusta, Georgia. Shaw has solicited the help of businesses that sell carpeting to send the used carpets to its recycling center.

> *In an age of growing concern about environmental impact, companies have to take responsibility for more of the chain, from R&D through manufacturing, marketing, distribution, and even recycling and reuse.*

These reverse supply chains are not a new idea in concept. Coca-Cola and other soft drink manufacturers created systems decades ago for collecting glass bottles from customers (and still do this in some areas, particularly in developing nations). But the reverse supply chain has become much more widespread, complex, and sophisticated. It is being applied to products, such as automobiles, with European automakers and regulators looking at ways to address all the diverse waste that remains at the end of an automobile's life.

As companies start focusing on improving these broader chains, they are finding ways to change product design and use different materials or minimize packaging to reduce waste. The design of products can facilitate reuse of components in new products or incorporate materials that are easier to recycle or reuse. The same holds true for packaging. Sometimes the best way to reduce overall impact at the end of the chain is to start at the beginning with creative redesign.

To recognize these opportunities, however, companies need to be able to look across the entire chain.

In the garment industry, the reverse supply chain is primarily operated independently of the manufacturers and retailers. Charitable organizations in the developed world collect secondhand clothing that entrepreneurs then export to the developing world for a second life. This is a complicated, low-margin, but profitable business. Could manufacturers and retailers take a broader view and begin collecting their own used clothing to export to new markets?

Not only are companies responsible for the entire supply chain, regardless of whether they own it, but the definition of that supply chain is expanding. This expanded cradle-to-grave-and-beyond view not only helps the environment and leads to happier customers, but it sometimes presents better solutions. It turns out that recycling carpet materials is now cheaper than purchasing new raw material, so it is a win-win for companies such as Shaw and for the planet.

A Broader View of the Business

In the old, round world, the primary role of business was seen as making profits for shareholders. This is the classic Milton Friedman argument, or the "shareholder view" of the firm. Although this is still key, the flat world, with its network connections, demands a broader view. This world pushes us more toward the "stakeholder view" that the business has to consider its impact on many stakeholders (such as employees, customers, suppliers, and communities) in addition to investors. With network orchestration, most of the business is done outside the company, processes are built around the customer, and work cuts across global borders and legal jurisdictions. This makes it nearly impossible for an enterprise to ignore "outside" stakeholders and be successful in the long run. Too much of the business takes place "outside" the company, and value creation comes increasingly from integration rather

> *If most of the business is done outside the company, it is nearly impossible for an enterprise to ignore "outside" stakeholders and be successful in the long run.*

than specialization. Value in the round world was created through competition, from fighting tooth and nail against other companies to win profits for the firm. Value in the flat world comes much more from collaboration or orchestration. Shareholder investments are just one part of this collaboration.

Networks do not exist in isolation. Every node in the network has connections with other networks. Networks are connected to networks. This means that ripple effects can come from one of these connected networks and move across the entire system. In the United States, McDonald's has to consider customers, regulators, the media, and public opinion in making decisions about what it might have seen as a separate network: the supply chain for making toys for Happy Meals. But with McDonald's as a participant in all these networks, these are now linked and actions in one affect the other. Given these interlinked networks, the implications of decisions and actions can be quite complex. Network orchestrators need to be acutely aware of all the networks they are a part of— either directly or indirectly—in making decisions about the design and activities of the network.

> *Every node in the network has connections with other networks. This means that ripple effects can come from one of these connected networks and move across the entire system.*

In the round world, the costs of working with other stakeholders, such as employees, suppliers, and distributors, were kept under tight rein. Managers treated business as a zero-sum game; by paying the least to employees, suppliers, and distributors, the company was left with the most profit. Companies might even have had an adversarial relationship with customers, seeking to maximize profits for the firm at the customers' expense. But as Peter Drucker pointed out decades ago, the "purpose of the business is to create a customer."[29] This is more true than ever in a flat world.

Focusing on corporate social responsibility might have once been seen as a distraction from the business goal of earning shareholder returns. Now it is an integral part of success. At the same time, we need to acknowledge the economic benefits that companies bring to developing regions. Some companies have taken the easy route of cutting off all business with factories that are not in compliance, but a more measured response is to work with factory owners to bring conditions into line with global standards. This preserves employment for workers who need this income to survive, while ensuring that they have good working conditions and that manufacturing processes have minimal impact on the environment. This process of improving conditions requires hands-on orchestration.

This can be a win-win situation. Just as companies can achieve greater customization and flexibility without sacrificing efficiency by using more flexible manufacturing processes, the goals of corporate social responsibility are not at odds with efficient production. In fact, the best-run factories require structures and controls that also contribute to better compliance with social and environmental codes. End consumers can get what they want while retailers and suppliers can still earn a healthy profit. This is the potential of the flat world.

Are You Ready for the Flat World?

- How can you ensure compliance of outsourced manufacturing and services without imposing rigid controls?
- What are the emerging demands of customers and end consumers, and how do they need to be addressed in your business?
- In particular, how are demands for social and environment responsibility reshaping your business?
- How can you ensure control of your supply chains without ownership?
- How can you use audits, education, and other tools to ensure compliance?
- How can you take a broader view of the firm to understand the many networks (economic, social, political, etc.) in which it operates?
- Given the need to take responsibility for the whole chain, what do you need to do next?

5

Empower "Little John Waynes" to Create a Big-Small Company

How does a large company act entrepreneurially and flexibly without losing control? How can it take advantage of the flat-world opportunities to act small—and the demand to do so—without sacrificing the benefits of being part of a large organization? Give business unit leaders the autonomy of "Little John Waynes" combined with the support of the larger organization.

In the old U.S. Westerns, John Wayne often played a cowboy under attack on the American frontier. He would lead his fellow pioneers to circle their wagons against an enemy attack and would stand in the middle shouting orders and shooting at the bad guys. With rugged independence, they would stand against the world. This is why Li & Fung refers to the entrepreneurial leaders who run its customer-facing businesses as "Little John Waynes." They take their wagon trains out into new business areas in search of opportunities, and they stand independently. They build and orchestrate networks. They are able to respond quickly to changes on the ground. On these frontiers, they live or die by their own abilities.

But the difference is that whereas John Wayne had to rely upon his own resources as he defended his wagons, these Little John Waynes have a supply of ammunition and other resources flowing through the middle of the circle of wagons. They have access to centralized back-office and middle-office support, as well as the financial resources and reputation of the large organization. These resources allow leaders to act like a small company but draw upon the resources of a big one—a big-small company. The Little John Waynes do not have to think about human resources, information technology (IT), and accounting on a day-to-day basis. They have the resources to pursue growth opportunities. At the same time these Little John Waynes also are close to customers and sharply focused on their own businesses. They operate like entrepreneurs. They can concentrate on establishing goals, setting strategy, growing the business, and serving the customers.

> *Whereas John Wayne had to rely upon his own resources as he defended his wagons, these Little John Waynes have a supply of ammunition and other resources flowing through the middle of the circle of wagons.*

These Little John Waynes are given autonomy to hire and fire and reorganize their organizations from day to day—sometimes necessary, with rapid changes in customer demands and regulations—although they coordinate their actions with other parts of the organization. A typical unit at Li & Fung run by a Little John Wayne might have 20 to 50 employees doing $20 million to $70 million annually and making a $3 million contribution to overhead. Li & Fung has 170 such divisions. They benefit from the company's large network of suppliers even as they shape their own networks to the demands of their customers. Sometimes the larger organization proposes a change, as happened with the closing of an office in Italy that several different divisions used. Even here, each of the Little John Waynes could have chosen to keep an operation open there.

The Perils of the Flat-World Frontier

In a flat world, with powerful IT systems, small companies are on a more level footing with large rivals. Any small firm with a DHL account can offer competitive global shipping of products. This is the age of guerilla companies, where arrows can come from almost any direction, from anywhere in the world.

With powerful software and outsourced processes, a small competitor can go head-to-head with a large one. Disney and Pixar have to be concerned about the "mini-Pixars" who can make quality movies on shoestring budgets. In network television, Disney also has to be concerned about developments such as YouTube, where individuals in front of their computers can post short films that attract more viewers than high-production-value network shows, such as *Lost*. Small companies can use third-party modern logistics and work process software to compete. The entrepreneurial leaders of these small firms know their clients' children's names and birthdays. They have only a few customers, and they cultivate and watch them closely. In this world, size is not necessarily an advantage.

> *With powerful software and outsourced processes, a small competitor can go head-to-head with a large one. In this world, size is not necessarily an advantage.*

Think about the early *Star Wars* movies: The tiny rebel jets could fly circles around the legs of the massive AT-AT Imperial Walkers (an intimidating armor-plated, four-legged transport and combat vehicle) and trip them up. At a certain size, it is easy for companies to lose touch with their customers and markets. It is easy to lose the visceral feel of interaction with competitors. This can lead to a crisis of innovation and customer responsiveness. Everything that percolates to top management is in the form of numbers, profit, and loss, so it is easy to lose the direct touch with the business that young startups have as a birthright.

Little John Waynes allow large companies to create their own flexible guerilla operations that are much more maneuverable and more resilient. Why not just break the company into many small pieces? Being part of a large organization still offers advantages. Entrepreneurs out on the frontier often become distracted by the operational demands of the business or run out of resources. Little John Waynes act like entrepreneurs within a large company.

By creating the Little John Waynes, the company focuses on business challenges instead of the functional approach that dominates in many large organizations. Instead of the independent fiefdoms of human resources, finance, legal and other areas, this structure ensures that senior leaders take interdisciplinary approaches to addressing the business issues of customers. The Little John Waynes draw upon functional expertise in this process but are able to integrate and focus this expertise. This ensures that the demands of functional areas do not predominate.

The Frontier Spirit

Who are these Little John Waynes? They do not wear boots and spurs. In fact, they are an incredibly diverse group of leaders. But they share a common entrepreneurial spirit. If they were not Little John Waynes, they would be building their own companies, as many of them did before becoming part of Li & Fung.

Tom Haugen, executive director of Li & Fung, contrasts the system to traditional companies. "I spent many years in large U.S. corporations and saw how dysfunctional and Dilbert-like they can be," he says. "Here we get a direction, and the job is to go and execute. Your ability to earn money is not restricted in any way. It is not dependent on anyone else's opinion other than the customer. It can be daunting for people who like rules—they come and leave quickly—but if you have just a tad of creativity and you can be ethical and legal, you can make money here."

It takes a certain kind of manager to thrive in this environment, and the Little John Wayne structure helps to attract and retain this type of manager. Many great managers typically are lost after acquisitions or mergers. The managers of the acquired businesses often feel stifled by an ill-fitting structure and culture of the parent firm. The Little John Wayne structure allows them to retain a degree of autonomy, which aids in the integration of the new business and the retention of skilled managers.

The Little John Waynes have the ability to test themselves in the trenches. They gain perspectives across the entire business instead of a small functional area. This is great preparation for assuming a broader role in the company. About 60 percent of Li & Fung's top management comes from acquired companies, so they bring an entrepreneurial spirit and independence to their work along with an understanding of how to successfully run their businesses. In selecting other people to fill these positions, it is important to bring in managers who are willing to take risks and to work independently.

Little John Waynes are self-starters who have the ability to make decisions and live with the consequences. Yet, they have to have the ability to operate within a broader organization.

> *Little John Waynes are self-starters who have the ability to make decisions and live with the consequences.*

Encashing and Incentives

To complement the entrepreneurial principle, Li & Fung emphasizes variable returns and a flexible compensation system to reward the senior ranks in the company. The Little John Waynes receive basic benefits such as insurance and retirement, but other perks are "encashed," which translates into dollar figures based on employees' performance during the year. Instead of offering a company car, Li & Fung translates that benefit into cash. This allows managers to choose their own car or use the funds for something else. It adds a clarity to compensation and incentives that is sometimes lost in the distribution of perks. Li & Fung believes this principle will empower staff to strive for excellence, which, in turn, provides high-level customer service. This makes the payoff from business success more direct and visible, as with being the owner of a smaller company.

In addition to offering cash rewards rather than perks, companies need to emphasize variable compensation to ensure that the interests of the Little John Waynes align with serving customers and growing the business. At Li & Fung, the percentage of variable compensation for Little John Waynes is an average 70 percent, with only 30 percent of compensation fixed. This means that these executives are largely rewarded based on their own performance. The upside is that the variable pay is never capped, unlike at many multinationals. The next level down, 60 percent of compensation is fixed and 40 percent is variable; at the third level, 80 percent is fixed and 20 percent is variable. The variable compensation is balanced between long term (stock options) and short term (profit sharing). The goal is for the top of each Little John Wayne organization to think and act like owner-entrepreneurs while enjoying the safety net of a large company. To do this, their compensation needs to be tied to the success of their businesses. When their customers win, they win.

Policies and Culture

With an autonomous structure, one of the potential pitfalls is to have rogue executives who are not aligned with the broader business. What keeps these rugged cowboys from taking the law into their own hands and taking the organization in directions it should not go, in the name of building their own businesses? Promoting independence and autonomy can be a dangerous game. Several mechanisms keep these independent leaders aligned with the broader organization. Processes for periodic review of the business units ensure that all managers examine their contributions to the overall enterprise, as we discuss in Chapter 6, "Establish the Three-Year Stretch to Balance Stability and Renewal." A strong culture across the business units also helps to keep managers aligned with corporate values. Companies also need to create a high level of transparency, so everyone can see the progress of the business in all areas. This makes it harder to hide problems.

Independent and entrepreneurial business units can become disconnected so that the different businesses do not learn from one another. At this point, the organization gains from entrepreneurial perspectives but fails to build synergies and capture knowledge and best practices across the business. In addition to building culture and policies that keep the Little John Waynes aligned with corporate goals, regular communications and meetings help to ensure knowledge sharing and cooperation across business units. Twice each year, Li & Fung's 400 top managers from around the world (including the Little John Waynes) fly to Hong Kong for a top management meeting. These meetings strengthen the culture and also allow managers to see the goals and achievements of their peers, using peer pressure to encourage continuous improvement and high achievement.

A recent survey of managers conducted by Wharton's SEI Center for Advanced Studies in Management found that more than half said training and retaining managers was their top concern for competing in a flat world. As the demands increase and talent remains in short supply, creating new structures that engage and energize managers is vital to keeping them in the organization and working at their best. The Little John Wayne structure can help to do this.

Creating Plug-and-Play Enterprises

Achieving growth and entrepreneurship requires modular systems so new acquisitions or organic growth can be integrated into the broader enterprise. Cisco Systems is well known for its acquisition and integration strategy. This strategy of rapid integration helped Cisco purchase and integrate 70 companies between 1992 and 2000. Cisco has a dedicated team focused on acquisitions. On the first day, the new employees are transferred to Cisco voice mail and given new computers and software, new signage, and new business cards. Even the soda machines and refreshment area are switched out. Because Cisco has put so much of its business on the Web, the company can more easily tie in newly acquired firms to its culture and processes. Standardized systems are critical to smooth acquisitions and rapid growth.

Cisco's aggressive acquisition strategy was reevaluated after the dot-com bust in 2001, but its capability to integrate new acquisitions is still widely admired and continues to be important to its success. After regrouping, Cisco has since completed a number of successful acquisitions, including the $500 million purchase of Linksys, allowing it to move into the consumer market, and the $6.9 billion acquisition of set-top box maker Scientific Atlantic in 2006.

Although it might be no surprise that a technology company can be a pioneer in this area, Li & Fung has shown a similar approach to an old-line business such as garment sourcing. This approach requires the appropriate technology and the modular structure to allow for a plug-and-play system.

To effectively integrate acquisitions, companies need more than technology. They also have to create plug-and-play cultures. Li &

Fung acquired one of its major competitors, Dodwell, a part of the Inchcape Conglomerate, in 1995. One of the significant risks to this acquisition was the difference in the two organizations' cultures. Dodwell, a typical British trading firm, was led primarily by Western expatriate managers; Li & Fung, on the other hand, was very much a Chinese family firm in culture, if somewhat "American business school" in its practices. As such, it did not easily dismiss employees; instead, it treated them as family. But as the company grew, the culture expanded. Li & Fung did not expect Dodwell businesses to just conform to its culture. Instead, it created an open culture that allows for differences under a common "umbrella culture." The best of Dodwell's culture was evaluated and adopted as part of the overall culture of the expanded group. Whereas some companies put managers from the central office in charge of new acquisitions, Li & Fung does not. Instead, its preference is to use existing management but bring them into this umbrella culture. This open architecture makes Li & Fung's top management feel a bit like the United Nations. This approach has led to very high retention rates of managers after acquisitions and creates opportunities to learn from the best practices of the acquired firm.

> *To effectively integrate acquisitions, companies need plug-and-play technology and systems, as well as a plug-and-play culture.*

This umbrella culture also gives some freedom to local offices, recognizing that Thai employees might not do things the same way Hong Kong employees do. Instead of imposing a culture on the overseas branches and acquired firms, Li & Fung allows overseas offices to develop their own management model that fits local circumstances, even while centrally managing core areas such as remuneration, incentive schemes, ethics, and compliance. The balance required is to have enough flexibility to allow diverse cultures to thrive—so that the broader organization can learn from them—but also enough structure so the entire organization is linked.

A plug-and-play culture allows the acquiring organization to identify and absorb the best practices of the acquired firm. With the Colby acquisition, Li & Fung modified the customer-centric approach to the business, which was core to its strategy. At the time, Colby had more of a customer and geographic matrix structure, while

Li & Fung had a more of a vertical structure by customer only. After the acquisition, Li & Fung reorganized around the Colby strategy, allowing shared resources in smaller countries. From major strategic and organizational innovations such as this to smaller changes such as the design of offices and showrooms, best practices of acquisitions are absorbed to improve the overall business.

With each new acquisition, the company must assess the best practices of the whole company. The goal should be to learn from the acquired businesses and then standardize the best practices so that the acquisition is not just of employees or customers, but also of knowledge. By keeping the company open while maintaining rigorous systems, the company can learn from the best practices of its acquired firms. If something is good, it should be systematized so it becomes policy for the whole group.

The Wagon Trains: The Back Office and Middle Office

The Little John Waynes are supported by a back office structure that keeps the supplies flowing so these entrepreneurial leaders can focus on meeting the needs of customers and fighting battles with competitors. The goal of the back office is to standardize processes and reap economies of scale; the goal of the front office is to ensure flexibility toward the market. Any company might be concerned about the organization of its back-office and middle-office functions; the network orchestrator needs to design these functions in ways that support the network view. This means that they have to be flexible, modular, "plug-and-play" systems that allow for scaling up or down or reshaping as the business changes, and they must support diverse businesses and networks.

> *The network orchestrator needs to design back-office and middle-office functions in ways that support the network view.*

Although Li & Fung's divisions are operated with a high level of autonomy, they still share common accounting, human resources, and IT systems. Strict operational and financial procedures also apply to the areas of inventory control, cash management, and information systems.

At Li & Fung, an operation support group (OSG) serves as the back-office base. OSG administers four functions: IT, finance, human resources, and general administrative services. OSG maintains the IT system that keeps the database of more than 8,300 factories around the world (about 3,000 of which are producing for its customers at any given time).

In financial control, OSG is very conservative and acts as the "central bank" that keeps track of all revenues. All cash flows are managed centrally through Hong Kong, and all letters of credit come to Hong Kong for approval and are then reissued by the central office. OSG also offers financing options to suppliers in each business unit, if needed by suppliers and authorized by customers, for buying raw materials and advancing payment for shipments.

Aside from performing IT and financial control, OSG acts as an in-house human resources provider, offering recruitment services, internal staff transfers and training. As indicated, OSG takes care of all the back-end needs so that business units can focus on their core competencies. OSG creates a flexible and powerful "socket" for the front-end units to plug into using the "plug-and-play" model.

Why Not Outsource?

Shouldn't these back-office functions be completely outsourced? Arguably, a network orchestrator should not be tying up resources to deal with issues such as accounting, human resources, or IT, which can be outsourced. In building its plug-and-play platform, Li & Fung's OSG systems are so integral to the success of the enterprise that they need to be directed from within the company. Many of the IT systems are proprietary systems that the company had to invent to meet specific customer needs. However, OSG often contracts with outsourcing partners in building modules in IT, accounting, and human resources that the company then integrates into its back-office platform.

Although 80 percent of these systems might be standardized, the company needs flexibility to customize the other 20 percent of systems that each business unit needs to optimize its performance. Some software programs might need to be tailored to the needs of specific businesses. A lot of this type of work is outsourced. In addition to serving the individual business units, this customization and use of outsourced partners can lead to innovations that can be incorporated in the standardized systems and shared with the rest of the organization. In this way, the standardized systems keep getting better.

The ability to build and tailor a plug-and-play enterprise is a core competency of Li & Fung. It enables the company to grow and acquire new firms, facilitate sharing information, and keep loosely linked businesses aligned with overall corporate goals.

Expanding into the Middle Office

In fact, Li & Fung has recently taken steps to realize further efficiencies and synergies by moving from the back office to the "middle office." Whereas back-office systems such as accounting can be largely standardized across the businesses, front-office functions (such as merchandising, product development, quality assurance, and quality control) generally require a high degree of customization for the specific business. This means limited opportunities for standardization. In fact, standardized approaches could be counterproductive by interfering with the business. But a gray area exists between the front office and back office where there is some opportunity for standardization and consolidation; in this "middle office," shipping and vendor compliance, for instance, can be brought together centrally.

For example, each division used to have its own shipping staff. How could the company realize the synergies across different shipping operations but at the same time be responsive to the specific needs of each division? Li & Fung began reorganizing this middle-office function for better coordination and efficiency across all its shipping. These new systems had to be created without shutting down the system. Transforming and consolidating Li & Fung's shipping has meant keeping an operation that ships more than US $8 billion in goods around the world up and running while completely reorganizing its structure. This was done in stages. The first involved moving all the shippers to a single location in Hong Kong, even though they continued to report to their original divisions.

Once they were in one location, these shippers began identifying challenges and best practices. For example, an immediate challenge was storing all the documents that the 200 employees involved in shipping generated. The entire group adopted the best practice of the shipping department in one division, which had gone to a paperless system, storing documents on disk. Li & Fung uses task forces to plan and implement the work and ensure that all the impacts of the transition are considered before, during, and after the transition. These task forces help to identify and implement best practice from all parts of the organization. Although they still service individual divisions on an individual basis, now that the shippers are located together, they have begun to bargain collectively for better freight rates and to deal with freight forwarders and shipping lines as one company instead of many small ones.

Facilitating Growth

A modular and scalable approach to the business supports rapid and sustainable growth. Li & Fung's plug-and-play structure achieves two goals. First, it supports the entrepreneurial Little John Waynes so they can focus on their core businesses. Second, the plug-and-play system allows for the rapid integration of newly acquired businesses, as the company grows.

> *A modular and scalable approach to the business supports rapid and sustainable growth.*

During the 1980s, Li & Fung extended its sourcing offices beyond Asia Pacific to reach the broader Asia and South Asia region, and then into regions such as Africa, Mediterranean Europe, and Latin America. The company also moved into other areas, such as retailing in Asia and brand management in the United States. A resilient plug-and-play platform can allow the organization to quickly seize opportunities for growth.

This approach has allowed Li & Fung to sustain remarkable growth in both revenue and profit through acquisitions and organic growth, as shown in Figure 5-1. Li & Fung's acquisition of rival Dodwell in 1995 transformed it from a regional trader to a multinational virtually overnight. Dodwell had a complementary global business, with a largely European customer base as well as sourcing offices in South Asia, Europe, the Mediterranean, and Latin America. This gave Li & Fung a more balanced portfolio, "completing the mosaic" of the business. The acquisition almost doubled Li & Fung's turnover and consolidated its leadership role in its business.. Li & Fung continued to take advantage of the broader supply chain network after the acquisition, to boost profit margins and diversify both its supplier and customer bases.

Li & Fung has since undertaken several more large acquisitions, with good results. During 1999–2000, it acquired Colby Group, Camberley, and Swire & Maclaine. These three acquisitions together contributed a total of 21 percent to the growth of Li & Fung's turnover. Matching the diversification into hard goods, Li & Fung acquired Janco Overseas Limited, a buying agent headquartered in Hong Kong, in 2002. The acquisition enabled the firm to further strengthen its penetration into the supermarket and hypermarket sector, where significant growth is occurring in the private-label non-food business.

With its successful acquisitions and integration of these companies, Li & Fung became more diversified in product mix, geographic coverage, and customer base, and enjoys sustainable economies of scale. The plug-and-play structure and the Little John Waynes business model facilitated the successful integration of these new parts of the business.

The Little John Wayne structure also helps retain experienced managers. The experienced managers from the Dodwell acquisition, for example, all chose to remain after the merger. The expectation at the time of the merger was that 20 to 30 percent of Dodwell's clients might be lost, yet none of them actually left.

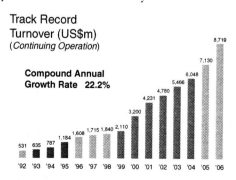

FIGURE 5-1   Li & Fung, Ltd., business performance

Li & Fung never stops evolving and growing. It was a US$1.2 billion company in 1995 and was an $8 billion business by 2006. Each stage of growth has required reinventing the company, and a flexible plug-and-play system has been critical in this rapid evolution. Although discussions have arisen about the limits of growth, companies such as Wal-Mart and Starbucks have continued to defy predictions that they will run out of room to grow. Some natural limits—people, capital, customers—might exist, but a world with global reach offers many advantages to companies that have the size and capabilities to capitalize on them. Large companies are actually able to grow faster than small ones if they have the ability to think small and create flexible businesses linked by plug-and-play systems.

Plug-and-play systems can streamline the process of growth. New businesses have immediate access to the knowledge and resources of the larger parent organization, while maintaining their individual identities. As with LEGO building blocks, this approach allows the company to build creatively and rebuild flexibly, to respond to customers better and improve the operation of the business.

How the West (and East) Were Won: Giving Wings to a Tiger

An old Chinese saying focuses on giving "wings to a tiger." With an entrepreneur, you have a tiger. The organization gives these tigers wings with technology, resources, scale, and other advantages of the large organization in a flat world. These winged tigers can go anywhere in the world and are nimble enough to compete with the smallest of competitors.

As the world becomes flatter, companies can either armor-plate themselves, creating a huge fortress of factories and closely linked suppliers, or break into smaller entrepreneurial units. Little John Waynes do both. They are free to work independently, close to the ground, to build independent businesses, but they also can draw upon the resources and knowledge of the overall enterprise. This system has married the strengths of being both small and big at the same time: Small and customer-centric business units can respond to customer needs fairly quickly, and at the back end, they enjoy the support of the company's powerful resources.

The Little John Wayne approach offers a way to encourage entrepreneurship within a large organization. Each small company is a growth company. Startups can grow much more

> *As the world becomes flatter, companies can either armor-plate themselves, creating a huge fortress of factories and closely linked suppliers, or break into smaller entrepreneurial units. Little John Waynes do both.*

rapidly than established firms. In a world where companies are looking for growth opportunities, this decentralized approach propels the overall organization ahead in ways that an organization cannot achieve if the entire company walks in lock step. The company combines the strengths of a large organization and the flexibility and innovation of a small one.

Are You Ready for the Flat World?

- In what ways does your current organization limit or dampen entrepreneurship?
- How could the organization be changed to embrace a "Little John Wayne" approach?
- What kind of incentives, hiring, and culture would you need to make this work?
- How can you adopt a plug-and-play approach that allows for growth and integration of new parts of the business?
- With more entrepreneurship, how do you maintain control over operations?
- What parts of the business can be handled most effectively by the back office and middle office?
- How can you use a plug-and-play system to drive growth, both organically and through acquisitions?
- Given the need to encourage and support entrepreneurial leaders in your organization, what do you need to do next?

6

Establish the Three-Year Stretch to Balance Stability and Renewal

In a flat world, companies need the flexibility to respond quickly to changes, but they also need enough stability so that managers can tell whether they are succeeding or failing. How can companies balance stability and renewal? For Li & Fung, it meant recognizing the combined wisdom of Western planning, stretch goals, and the fixed plans of China's centrally planned economy.

Almost monthly, Spencer Fung, who runs the Gymboree business at Li & Fung, rearranges its organizational charts and the desks and cubicles in his division. In pursuit of stretch goals that are part of the overall company's three-year plan, there is no standing still. Industry and customer demands shift quickly, so there is a constant need for renewal. At the same time, stability is crucial to success in a business based on long-term relationships with customers.

In a flat world that is rapidly changing, companies need to balance stability and renewal. How do organizations plan in a way that allows for renewal but also creates enough stability so entrepreneurial units know where they stand? How do companies in a flat world balance the need to motivate their divisions to move toward a common goal with the freedom to allow them to respond to immediate changes in their business environments? The solution for Li & Fung has been to develop a planning process that creates stretch goals that are renewed every three years. In this rapidly changing world, five-year plans are too long and one-year budgets are too short to build anything meaningful. Three years seem to be just the right duration. This pushes independent divisions to change and renew their strategies and organizations, while giving them a sufficient period of time to achieve these goals. All the parts of the organization are on the same page, but enough space exists for individual business leaders to rearrange the desks in their offices.

> *In a flat world that is rapidly changing, companies need to balance stability and renewal. Five-year rolling plans can create a moving target, but yearly budgets are too short to build anything meaningful.*

The Problem with Moving Targets

Classical Western business planning, the approach taught in most business schools, tends to be done on a rolling basis. Each plan might nominally last for five years, but because the plan is changed each year, or even more frequently, the actual goals are a moving target. The targets often shift just when managers have spent the first year preparing for the original plan. Pressure from financial markets and these shifting long-term plans tend to fix the focus on short-term results, with many firms concentrating their attention on the next quarter. Although rolling plans allow the organization to respond more rapidly to changes in the environment, it can make it hard for leaders in the organization to set and maintain a course.

In contrast, the Chinese Communist central planning was done in its famous fixed five-year intervals. The grand plan was announced at the start of the period. Everyone knew where the country was headed and the goals it needed to reach over the five years. The whole nation then focused on it until the next plan was achieved. This seems at first like an unnaturally rigid process for a world that can undergo extreme changes in five years. Yet there is wisdom to this approach. Just as early mariners used fixed stars to find their way to port, this fixed set of goals gives everyone a context in which to work.

Li & Fung's planning combines the best of Chinese central planning and Western planning theory. Like the Chinese central planning system, the plans are fixed. The goals stay the same throughout the entire three-year period. Like however, Western management theory, each plan starts with a clean slate (is zero-based), and the process involves scenario forecasting and backward planning. Although there is centralized goal setting, there is no centralized execution. Individual business leaders determine how they will reach their goals in the allotted period.

> *Li & Fung's planning combines the best of Chinese central planning and Western planning theory.*

A zero-based and fixed plan every three years takes more time and effort to formulate, but it allows management to analyze the environment and assess the company's potential regardless of previous activities and results. Nothing is sacrosanct, so it creates a sense of renewal.

Stability and Renewal

The three-year plan avoids the tendency with rolling plans for managers not to take the plans seriously (they will change next year) or to begin laying the foundation for one plan, only to have the direction change in the next year. Once developed, the fixed, three-year plan is cast in stone and stays unchanged for the duration. During the first year, the company adopts and starts implementing the plan. In the second year, the whole company concentrates on executing the plan. The plan is completed and reviewed in the third year.

Stability is needed to build relationships. Although we compete in a flat world, relationships are disrupted by constant reorganization and high staff turnover. It takes years to develop relationships with customers and suppliers. The first two years with a new customer, in a new country, or with new suppliers are typically fraught with problems until the bugs are worked out. This demands some stability in the organization. As the world is getting smaller, reputation matters more. In a flat world where technology and business models change rapidly but relationships, regulations, and business move more slowly, companies need to reorganize their cubicles overnight but still maintain an engaged network.

Although the three-year timeframe works for Li & Fung, each business needs to select the time period that is best suited to its own cycles. A fast-moving business might need tighter cycles. Other companies do best with five-year plans. The important thing is to select a time period that provides enough stability to implement new strategies, restructure organizations to execute these new strategies, complete key projects, and achieve stretch goals.

The Power of the Stretch

Instead of traditional incremental annual targets, the three-year planning at Li & Fung is built around ambitious stretch goals that are set in collaboration with the "Little John Waynes" leading individual business units. Stretch goals require a shift in thinking, the adoption of new mental models. Mental models constrain opportunities for individuals and organizations, so changing these models can open new opportunities. For example, when Roger Bannister proved that it was possible to run the four-minute mile in 1959, 16 runners broke this once-impenetrable barrier within three years.[30] This result was not through a breakthrough in human evolution, but rather a breakthrough in thinking. Bannister no longer saw the four-minute mile as an insurmountable barrier. This impossible feat was now considered possible. Stretch goals force executives to think creatively about their own mental models.

> *Stretch targets result not only in transformation of the business, but in tremendous gains in performance.*

These strategic plans become drivers for innovation, improved performance, and growth. For example, in the early 1990s, Li & Fung set a goal of doubling its profits, which could not easily be achieved through organic growth. This led to an exploration of alternatives for reaching the goals, which resulted in an acquisitions strategy. In the

1996–1998 three-year plan, Li & Fung grew rapidly by acquiring Dodwell and integrating the company into the organization.

More recent plans have taken the company and its divisions in new directions (see Figure 6-1). The 1999–2001 plan for Li & Fung's Integrated Distribution Services (IDS) business addressed the challenge of managing change and creating a new culture. The primary focus was on operations excellence to build customer accounts and regional relationships. The most important outcome of this change process was the establishment of logistics as a leading core business of the IDS group. The next three-year plan (2002–2004) redefined the business in the face of emerging competition. The first plan was about how to do things better; this one was about how to do things differently. By the end of 2004, IDS had emerged as a totally different company, having fundamentally changed its business model. The end of the plan also saw the achievement of the goal to list IDS on the Hong Kong Stock Exchange. The next plan (2005–2007) recognized that much remained to be done for IDS to continue to lead in the distribution industry transformation. How could it implement its business model faster, better, deeper, and wider?

The result is not only transformation of the business, but tremendous gains in performance. Between 2002 and 2006, IDS achieved compound annual revenue growth of above 20 percent, and net operating profit rose by 67 percent. By the end of 2006, IDS had strengthened its leadership in logistics in China, with coverage across 120 cities.

Other companies have also used stretch goals to propel their progress. For example, when leading U.S. public relations firm MS&L set a stretch goal in 1997 to triple its revenues from $33 million to $100 million in five years, it needed to change its thinking about the business. At the time, the mental model of the industry was based on a tactical and transactional approach. Achieving the stretch goal meant rethinking the firm to take a more strategic focus on a total integrated marketing communications strategy. Instead of running a series of baby races for the diaper brand of a major consumer packaged goods company, the agency would help design, implement, and manage strategic marketing communications across the firm's many product lines and businesses worldwide. The stretch goal was a catalyst for changing the agency's thinking because the company could not reach this goal by doing what it had in the past. MS&L, now part of Publicis Groupe, achieved its $100 million goal in just three years.

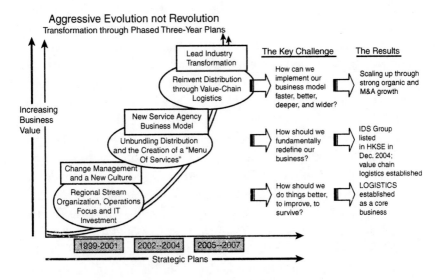

FIGURE 6-1   A series of three-year plans for Li & Fung's IDS division illustrates how the plans drive growth, address key business challenges, and set stretch targets for results. These goals then drive a series of transformations that increase value.

Investment firm SEI has set a series of stretch goals that have led to rapid growth and rethinking of the business. It has undergone a number of transformations as it has grown from a small startup in 1968 to a leading provider of investment accounting and administrative services, processing more than $50 trillion of investment transactions annually, administering $320 billion in mutual fund and pooled assets, and managing more than $135 billion in investments. SEI operates 22 offices in 12 countries and is a perennial member of *Fortune's* list of "Best Companies to Work for in America." Its goals have moved it from providing software systems for trust departments to outsourcing treasury and other services, and most recently to providing integrated solutions for financial wellness. The "financial wellness" service for high-net-worth individuals is designed to do what the Mayo Clinic does in treatment with a team of medical experts. SEI is bringing together a set of financial and life planners to look at estate planning, investments, insurance, and life goals. This has allowed the company not only to achieve rapid growth, but also to keep ahead of the "commoditization demon," in the words of founder and CEO Al West. As he says, "You cannot grow the bottom line in the long run if you don't find ways to grow the top line."

The power of such stretch goals has often been demonstrated in product development. When Canon set about creating the personal copier, the demand that it could be maintained by individual owners and sold for less than $1,000 forced designers to develop the radical innovation of a low-cost, disposable cartridge. The stretch goal created a new model for copiers and opened up new markets for small businesses.

Similarly, when designers were challenged by the resource constraints of emerging markets, they were forced to rethink their approaches and were able to come up with innovations such as a $100 prosthetic leg. This would not have been possible without challenging their mental models.

The whole concept of backward planning incorporating stretch goals emerged from what Russell Ackoff refers to as "idealized design."[31] Instead of starting at the present and working forward to a future state, typically an incremental route, idealized design starts with a desired future state and works backward to the actions necessary to achieve it. For example, Ackoff describes how he attended a meeting at Bell Laboratories in 1951. The vice president of Bell Labs announced one morning at a meeting for section heads that the telephone system in the United States had been destroyed the night before. It became clear that this was fiction, but it still was jarring enough to allow the engineers to take a fresh look at redesigning the system from scratch. This "idealized design" process led to some of the most significant modern innovations in the phone system, including TouchTone phones, call waiting, call forwarding, voice mail, caller ID, conference calls, speaker phones, speed dialing, and mobile phones.

Where's the Stick?: No Penalties for Falling Short

What happens if a business leader does not achieve the stretch goal? No heads will roll. Many long-time Li & Fung managers have missed one or two stretch goals. They are still with the organization. Incentives are tied to achieving business results, but no specific incentives are tied to achieving the final goal of the three-year plan. This might seem counterintuitive because managers would be expected to achieve goals only if their incentives were appropriately aligned. If you don't pay for results, won't managers ignore these plans?

The problem is that if all or the bulk of incentives were linked to achieving the final target of the plan, managers would not be willing to stretch. They would think incrementally and game the system to make sure they received their performance bonus. But there are no penalties for missing a plan. It is a stretch goal. By definition, it is possible but not easily achievable, which means there is a high risk of failure. Top management at Li & Fung firmly believe that the company will achieve better results by setting stretch targets that might not be achieved than following a system that encourages conservative and "safe" targets.

> *No incentives are tied to the three-year plan because it would encourage managers to think incrementally and game the system.*
> *Instead, incentives are for growth.*

This approach might seem more carrot than stick. It is designed to motivate and empower business leaders. But what keeps them engaged in meeting these goals? Incentives *are* aligned with growth. Managers are rewarded on incremental performance on their business. Additional incentives are awarded if executives meet or exceed their stretch goals. But if managers fall slightly short of the goal, they are still rewarded for the successful performance of their business.

In addition, peer pressure within the organization focuses on achieving growth objectives. Twice a year, all the leaders of the businesses from all around the world meet and present reports on progress toward their three-year plans. This means that six times during a three-year plan, the heads of the business streams are called to account. This can be a powerful force in focusing attention on the three-year plans. No one wants to have to explain a poor report at one of these meetings.

Measuring stretch goals and holding managers accountable can be a powerful force in focusing attention on them. New York City Mayor Rudolph Giuliani and Police Commissioner William Bratton transformed the city's police department using measurement and reporting as a key mechanism for "challenging every single assumption about urban policing."[32] New York began measuring crime patterns more effectively in real time using the equivalent of a dashboard and holding individual leaders accountable for the results. This continuous, quantitative measurement and reporting process helped drive changes in thinking and behavior.

On the other hand, what happens if you achieve your three-year goal in one year? In some organizations, if you meet your goals this year, the bar is raised the next. But with the fixed plan, the bar stays in the same place. A business that has met its goals early can then relax. The group that achieves these stretch goals early has the luxury of regrouping, training, or taking advantage of a slow time after an intense stretch to consolidate and avoid "burnout." This is vital to building new capacities and balancing growth and consolidation.

> *A business that has met its goals early can then relax. It has the luxury of regrouping, training, or taking advantage of a slow time after an intense stretch to consolidate and avoid "burnout."*

Formulating the Plan

The plans are formulated by examining the company's own markets and business, as well as the external environment. They are developed from the bottom up and top down in an iterative process. The process is initiated from the top of the organization but becomes a dialogue between the insights of leaders of business units and the goals of the broader organziation. A tension exists between goals that are easily achieved and others that are more difficult to accomplish. The planning process typically goes through the following steps, illustrated in Figure 6-2.

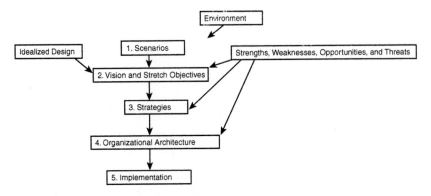

FIGURE 6-2   Formulating the three-year plan

1. Paint Scenarios for the Next Three Years

Plans must be based upon the current environment and an understanding of how it will evolve in the future. The first step in formulating the three-year plan is to imagine the situation three years down the road. By analyzing trends, management can paint a scenario for the business environment. The analysis reflects the macroeconomic situation, regulatory trends, the market for suppliers and customers, research on market trends, and the impact of technology in a business context. The scenarios also need to take into consideration the interactions among the different trends and uncertainties. Many forces are shaping and reshaping the flat world, and the first step in developing a three-year plan is to examine these forces and see where they might lead.

In the 1999–2001 three-year plan for Li & Fung, for example, the environmental analysis considered respective trends of customers' markets (the U.S., Europe, and Japan) and those of the sourcing markets (the Chinese mainland and Asia after the financial crisis), the impact of currency fluctuations such as the inception of the euro, new international trade rules, new technology, and rivalry within the industry. Every factor that could affect business was considered both at the macro level and at more micro levels.

2. Set a Vision and Stretch Objectives

In many cases, companies with established operations tend to stay in their comfort zones. The purpose of stretch objectives is to make managers and employees uncomfortable, to push them to do more than they think is possible. This process of creating a stretch creates a problem that cannot be solved using the current mindset, and this encourages managers to come up with innovative solutions.

The company's vision guides the development of its plans for long-term growth. The overall vision and mission of the company guide the process of creating stretch objectives. The mission of Li & Fung is to be the premier global consumer products trading company, "delivering the right product to the right place at the right time at the right price." Just as the scenarios provide the external context for planning, the vision and mission provide the internal context. Whatever plans are developed need to be consistent with this overall vision and mission.

Both the environment and the firm itself determine the resulting vision. It represents the convergence of the type of company that will be successful under the evolving environment and the organization's own aspirations.

3. Use Backward Planning to Develop Strategies to Bridge Gaps

By their nature, stretch goals often do not have a clear path when they are established. This results in creative thinking about how to get from here to there, using the planning approach of "idealized design" to build a path to an idealized future, as discussed earlier. The process of idealized design leads to a set of strategies and action plans for achieving the stretch goals. The path is often very different from the one that has taken the company to this point in its development. If stretch objectives point out the destination on a map, then backward planning is a method of identifying the gap between the origin and the destination. Performing SWOT (strengths, weaknesses, opportunities, and threats) analysis can help identify the gaps. It also demonstrates what strengths and opportunities are available for achieving the goals. At the same time, idealized design identifies the weaknesses that the company should tackle and the potential threats that it should anticipate. The results of the SWOT analysis can help the company discover ways to achieve the planned goals.

4. Develop the Organizational Architecture

These broad strategies must be supported by an organizational architecture. Stretch objectives might require changes to many different aspects of organizational architecture, including culture, structure, processes, governance, people, resources, technology, incentives, and performance measures. Without these changes, it can be very difficult, if not impossible, to translate stretch objectives into successful action. All of these elements of architecture are interdependent, so they need to be designed to support one another.

5. Create an Implementation Plan

Finally, the strategies need to be translated into a specific implementation plan. Where are resources needed? Where can they be cut back? What are the milestones for measuring progress? It is important to assign senior managers to supervise the progress of each step of the implementation process and coordinate cross-departmental efforts. In Li & Fung's 1999–2001 three-year plan, executive directors were each in charge of a specific strategy in addition to their daily operational responsibilities. These implementation plans should follow the approach of adaptive experimentation, experiments that can be reassessed and adjusted along the way based on outcomes and changes in the business environment.

Planning for Networks

In designing its plans for the future, the network orchestrator has to pay particular attention to the design and development of its networks. What networks need to be built or expanded to fulfill these objectives and meet the changing demands posed by scenarios for the future? Part of achieving stretch growth targets involves creating the networks that can deliver this growth. The network orchestrator needs to create these networks organically or through acquisitions. The growth of the business demands growing the network.

In designing its plans for the future, the network orchestrator has to pay particular attention to the design and development of its networks. What networks need to be developed to fulfill these objectives and meet the changing demands posed by scenarios for the future?

Partners in the network also need to be aligned with the overall vision for the company and its growth objectives. Individual suppliers need to see how the company's overall growth can benefit their own growth and development. The overall vision for the company drives the overall development of the network.

Plans for growth of the businesses and networks should be designed to fill in missing capabilities and strengthen weaknesses of the organization, to "fill out the mosaic." Venture capital and acquisitions should be used strategically to build organizational capabilities. For example, if Li & Fung is relatively weak in ladies' fashion shoes, its venture group might find an entrepreneurial company with people who can create great designs and marketing but who have few sourcing or production capabilities. Li & Fung invested in Cyrk to build strengths in the promotional premiums business, (clothing or gift items with promotional logos). Li & Fung bought a 30 percent stake for $200,000 in 1990, created a line of promotional clothing for Philip Morris and others, and sold the investment for $65 million about five years later. The Dodwell acquisition, as discussed earlier, complemented Li & Fung's positions in the U.S. and Asia with a stronger footprint in Europe. By taking a deliberate approach to acquisitions and growth, companies can use acquisitions to deliberately flesh out the big picture for their enterprises and provide access to the networks needed to succeed in the future.

A New Organization Every Three Years

One Li & Fung manager compared the three-year stretch goals to working for a new organization every three years. Instead of changing companies, he could stay at the same firm for decades but feel like he was working at a new company every three years. By renewing the business, the company also offers managers the opportunity for professional renewal, taking on a fresh challenge.

One Li & Fung manager compared the three-year stretch goals to working for a new organization every three years.

This could make managers more paranoid and creates uncertainty because often the exact path to the stretch goal is unknown at the outset. It creates a challenge, forcing managers to make their own employees uncomfortable. But because this renewal occurs in discrete periods, they have enough stability to actually make gains in reaching their stretch goals.

The three-year plan can also be applied to personal goals. For example, William Fung created a personal three-year plan to run a marathon. Beginning in his mid-50s, and with a build he describes as more like a wrestler than runner, it was certainly a true stretch goal. He took a disciplined approach to achieving the goal, slowly expanding his range until he was able to run the marathon. Without even working with a trainer, such a goal is a very lonely and personal journey that he considers one of his finest achievements. This was an achievement that was based on his own discipline and initiative. Within three years, at the age of 57, he ran across the finish line of the London Marathon, a true stretch in many ways.

Companies have to reinvent themselves periodically to create what former Royal Dutch/Shell executive Arie de Geus calls "living companies." In Li & Fung's case, this process of reinvention occurs in three-year cycles. Planning in the fast-moving flat world needs to be renewed to reflect a changing world yet still provide enough stability so that managers can make plans and implement them. The temptation in a world of rapidly flowing information and a shifting environment is to respond to every shift in the winds. A ship that responds to every change of winds will never reach its port. Instead, the captain needs to set a course, get all the crew focused on heading toward it, and then periodically reassess the position and make corrections. The goals are decided centrally, but how managers reach them depends on their local creativity. Using fixed three-year plans, the organization keeps everyone on the same page but gives business leaders extreme flexibility in meeting these goals.

Are You Ready for the Flat World?

- What is the right planning cycle for your business? One year? Three years? Five years?
- How would moving from a rolling plan to a zero-based, fixed plan change your business?
- Does your planning balance stability with renewal?
- Are you using stretch objectives? What stretch objectives could inspire employees to change their thinking and develop innovative approaches?
- How can you use idealized design to create stretch objectives?
- What changes to organizational architecture and implementation plans are needed to achieve these stretch goals?
- What incentive systems and processes are required to ensure that managers take stretch goals seriously but do not become too timid in setting them?
- Given the need to balance stability and renewal in your planning, what do you need to do next?

7

Build the Company
Around the Customer

*How can companies put the customer at the center without
giving up their own identity, organization, and profitability?
Freed from owning factories, the orchestrator can create
the supply chain and the business around the customer.
Companies and their customers are bound together by thick
connections, a combination of human relationships, business
processes, and technology.*

U.S.-based children's retailer Gymboree has a staff of more than 200
people who source its clothing from some 150 factories in 12 countries. A large headquarters is located in Hong Kong, and sourcing
teams are in the Philippines, Indonesia, and China. But most of these
sourcing employees do not work for Gymboree: Despite the Gymboree logos in the office, they work for Li & Fung. Each of the
employees has a computer linked directly to Gymboree. Gymboree
managers can log onto a website bearing its logo and check the status
of its orders, but the site resides on Li & Fung's computers. With the
help of technology and an organization focused around the customer,
the lines between companies have begun to blur.

The orders for Gymboree garments come in four or five times per year, with more than 2,000 styles per season. The information is sent out to factories for specifications and samples. Each manager considers a few hundred items and determines the best locations in the world for producing them. The details of tricky embroidery are worked out through samples shuttled back and forth between Li & Fung, suppliers, and Gymboree. One card with samples of fine needlework for a single child's blanket contains faux suede, embroidery, appliqué, and crochet images of dogs. All these different techniques made the product quite complex; it took several rounds with the factory in Thailand to get everything perfect. The manager might get quotes for projects from three or four different factories, often in different countries. Then, based on price, quality, and other factors, the manager can determine the best supply chain for the specific order.

Launching a New Business

The flexibility of this network was apparent when Gymboree began planning to launch a new upscale brand for babies to toddlers in 2002. It needed to develop an entirely new line of clothing that was distinct from its Gymboree line. It began discussions with Li & Fung about the idea that became the very successful Janie and Jack shops. Li & Fung's broad network of suppliers helped identify factories with the expertise for hand-embroidery, hand-smocking, and vintage prints, as well as fabrics such as fine linens and cashmere that made the new line distinctive. They needed vendors who could supply the quality of 14 stitches per inch, considerably higher than most standard garments. Finally, they needed to find factories that were the right size to work on relatively small order quantities of 300 to 500 units per given style, orders that often are not attractive to very large factories.

Li & Fung identified a set of 20 factories that could handle the new line and also made suggestions about new fabrics. Since the launch of Janie and Jack in 2004, the new initiative has grown to more than 70 shops throughout the United States.

Li & Fung's extensive network of dispersed manufacturing also helps navigate shifts in consumer demands or helps in experiments with items beyond fashion. For example, Li & Fung helped Gymboree source non-garment specialty items, such as children's watches and umbrellas that are sold at its stores. Because of synergies with other divisions, Li & Fung was able to source relatively small quantities of umbrellas on behalf of Gymboree.

For the customer, the arrangement offers one-stop shopping. "We are able to send all our products over to one agency," says Mike Mayo, senior vice president of Gymboree. "They go into the Li & Fung's computer system and then are sent out to all of their locations throughout the world, whether they are in Indonesia, Bangkok, New Delhi, or Seoul. The different factories compete and get their costs as sharp as they can for a particular area."

The needs of customers might change, but a flexible organization with a flexible supply network can reconfigure itself to meet the changes of its customers. In a flat world, supply chains change. The product lines change. Whole new brands and businesses might be launched. The network is reconfigured in response. The only fixed point is the relationship with the customer at the center.

> *Customer needs might change, but a flexible organization with a flexible supply network can reconfigure itself to meet the changes of its customers.*

Customers Evoking Supply Chains

A word about customers and end consumers: For Li & Fung, the customer is typically a retailer or brand owner such as Gymboree that sells its products to end consumers. In these relationships, the network orchestrator needs to pay attention to immediate customers as well as end consumers. The tastes and demands of these consumers shape the products needed by retailers. The transparency of the flat world can connect the network orchestrator with both the direct customer and the end consumer, and even connect suppliers with data from the checkout at the end of the supply chain. Whereas Li & Fung's businesses are built around its retail customers, a company that sells directly to end consumers might develop similar networks with consumers at the center.

The network is built around the potential needs of current and future customers. A supply chain is evoked from this network based on the needs of a specific customer such as Gymboree. In customization for end consumers, the supply chain might be designed to deliver a product for a single end customer. The customization available now is primarily relatively minor adjustments in size and fit or monogramming, but as technology improves and connections throughout the network advance, more opportunities could arise for deeper customization (a customer designs a dress online and has it delivered). As customization becomes more important, this customization for the end consumer has implications for the design of supply chains for retailers who serve these consumers.

> *The network is built around the potential needs of future customers. A specific supply chain is evoked from this network based on the needs of a specific customer.*

The addition of a network orchestrator might appear to add more cost to the system by adding another layer to the process, but better coordination and access to a broader network of suppliers can make the process more efficient and cost-effective for customers. These improvements can be seen in Li & Fung's 2006 agreement to take over international sourcing for KarstadtQuelle AG, Europe's leading department store and mail order company. (The deal included Li & Fung's acquisition of KarstadtQuelle's international sourcing operations with more than 1,000 employees.) It was expected to result in many improvements to the business, including a €500 million reduction in working capital, a reduction in purchase prices of 10 percent, a prolongation of payment terms, strategic advantages through faster collection cycles, and a strengthening of KarstadtQuelle's private labels. The arrangement also provided a scaleable platform for a planned doubling of import volume to €2 billion.

Cosourcing with Customers

The old supply chains started with the supplier, someone with a factory with capacity or products to sell; in the flat world, the supply chain begins with the customer. The rest of the chain is organized around the customer. Li & Fung has moved from a supply-centric model to a customer-centric model.

Li & Fung's coordinated suppliers' network and dedicated customer-oriented teams provide manufacturing and sourcing information around the world to customers, match customers' production needs with factories' capabilities, supervise production and quality control, and do everything in accordance with trade restrictions. Once built, the relationship becomes much more fluid and allows for early collaboration in developing a new season or a new line. For example, one large customer might come to Li & Fung and say, "For next season, this is what we're thinking about—this type of look, these colors, and these quantities. Can you come up with a production program?"

Starting with the designers' sketches, Li & Fung researches the market to find the right type of yarn and dye swatches to match the colors. The company then can create an entire program for the season, specifying the product mix and the schedule. Li & Fung contracts for all the resources. It works with factories to plan and monitor production to ensure quality and on-time delivery.

Li & Fung provides the convenience of a one-stop shop for customers through a total value-added package: from product design and development; through raw material and factory sourcing, production planning and management, quality assurance, and export documentation; to shipping consolidation. The most important of these services involve monitoring suppliers' work on customers' orders to ensure quality and on-time delivery.

Most companies talk about being customer-centric. Some global firms such as IBM have moved to account strategies or matrix strategies focused on the customer instead of organizing around their own internal functions or geography. Li & Fung has about 170 customer-centric divisions, each focusing on one customer or a related group of customers. Each division averages about $20 million to $70 million annually. This helps keep each customer-centric division small and entrepreneurial.

These divisions exist to serve the customer. From the customer's perspective, these customer units are a form of outsourcing—or, more accurately, cosourcing. They are reorganized when customer needs shift and are disbanded if the customer leaves, although this is rare. The success and profit of each division are wholly tied to the success of a customer so that customer has their undivided attention.

As noted, Li & Fung still has regional branch offices but uses them differently than traditional trading companies. Other trading companies typically are organized geographically, with branch offices in each country serving as profit centers and competing against each other. Li & Fung does not calculate the profit and loss based on its individual branch offices. Instead, managers in branches are rewarded for their contributions to the overall success of the business instead of the success in their limited part of the world. As a result, branch office managers do not have a strong incentive to obtain orders solely for their own branch office; they can impartially decide which branch office is most capable to handle a particular order. In fact, many orders are fulfilled with one branch providing the raw materials and another branch supervising the actual production or assembly. Managers have no incentive to take a parochial view that might suboptimize the entire chain.

Understanding and Anticipating Customers

The success of the relationship with customers depends fundamentally on understanding their vision, their strategies, their organization, and the needs of their end consumers. The customer-centric organization needs to understand the needs of target market segments to select the best positioning and value proposition for their portfolio of segments. If a company's strategy is built around low cost, such as at Wal-Mart, this affects its sourcing decisions and supply chains. If a company is driven by design, as with Ralph Lauren, with the brand reflecting the person who wears it, price might be less important than finding just the right buttons, fabric, and styling. To truly build around the customer, you need to understand the customer's organization and strategy.

As the relationship develops, the customer-centric company not only should be *responsive* to customers, but should actually *anticipate* customer needs and the needs of their end consumers. Li & Fung serves as eyes and ears for its large customers, offering design services and monitoring consumer trends. Li & Fung staff visit "fashion cities" such as Paris and Milan every season to learn the latest market trends and fashion concepts. At the start of every quarter of the year, the procurement staff of Li & Fung visits its major suppliers, providing them with the latest fashion trends. Li & Fung even publishes a "fashion trend report" for its clients every February and September. This can provide an early-warning system for shifts in the industry. In return, its suppliers provide the Li & Fung staff with information about the procurement of different types of fabrics and components.

> *As the relationship develops, the customer-centric company not only should be responsive to customers, but should actually anticipate customer needs and the needs of their end consumers.*

Increasing Customization

Expectations keep rising. End consumers expect increased customization without significant increases in cost. Costs have continued to rise in almost every other area, yet prices have been held down in the garment industry through process and location innovations in manufacturing, such as those pioneered by Li & Fung, reducing cost while increasing flexibility and quality. Large retailers, such as Wal-Mart, also have consolidated buying power into fewer hands. Low costs must be achieved without sacrificing quality, and there is increased demand for better quality with the emergence of mass luxury items in many categories. Intensified competition has led to rapid commoditization, demanding faster innovation to differentiate products and keep up with changing consumer tastes.

Empowered end consumers now expect the mass customization and instantaneous response of the Internet, for products from customized computers to designer jeans. They know what they want, they want it exactly, and they want it now. More businesses are becoming time-sensitive, not only in the fashion arena, but in areas such as food and high-tech consumer products. Clothing retailers are working with six or seven seasons a year instead of just two or three, making fashion retailing a more dangerous game. This has increased the value of fast and flexible supply chains that can be reconfigured up to the last minute to respond to the changing tastes of end consumers.

> *Empowered end consumers now expect mass customization and instantaneous response.*

The move to customization has also led to a fragmentation of markets. These smaller markets add to uncertainty. Once the whole ocean is broken into small ponds, these smaller ponds are more responsive to small shocks. Ripples move through them more quickly, so these niche markets add to uncertainty. Companies need systems to respond effectively to these volatile segments, or they face increased risks of markdowns when demand changes. Line changes that took days or weeks now have to be achieved in hours or minutes. This need for flexibility erodes the advantages of scale in manufacturing and gives more advantage to small manufacturers, leading to the democratization of the supply chain.

Engaging in Co-Development

Although Li & Fung's customers are retailers and brand managers, products ultimately go to end consumers. Changes in the relationship of companies to consumers are transforming product development, marketing, and production. One of the advantages of working more closely with customers is that they can become true partners in code-velopment. In studying innovation in many industries, Eric Von Hipple of MIT and colleagues found that many important innovations were developed first by users.[33] The role of users varies by industry. Some 90 percent of innovations in engineering plastics come from manufacturers, while 77 percent of innovations in scientific instruments come from users. A study at 3M found that products based on user innovation were eight times more successful than manufacturer-based products. On average, users developed early prototypes five to seven years before manufacturers started working on these innovations. For example, an automated radioimmunoassay system for medical research initially was rigged up by a lab researcher who needed to complete a study that required 20,000 assays.

Users and other partners need to be invited into the network. eBay initially took a narrow view of its relationship to its network of programmers, charging fees to independent developers who created complementary software for its online auctions. When eBay abandoned the fees in 2005, the number of outside developers working on eBay-related software exploded from 300 to more than 3,000.[34] By engaging these developers, eBay has tapped into the creativity of a network of thousands of software developers who have created more than 4,000 independent programs. These independent programs, such as a program that allows buyers without a computer to bid easily over the phone, are used in about a quarter of eBay's listings. The company has even created a website, a newsletter, a discussion forum, software tools, and a conference for developers. By actively cultivating and expanding this network—engaging in network orchestration instead of taking a narrow view of the firm—eBay has built value for itself, outside developers, and its customers.

Companies such as Lego and Texas Instruments have discovered the value of engaging customers as cocreators of products. Texas Instruments has tapped into the insights of teachers in launching new calculators. When the Lego programmable robotics product called Mindstorms was launched for children 8 to 12, it took company engineers seven years to build the product. Within three weeks, hacker-customers were working on upgrades. It became an unexpected hit among customers who were over 18 and were actively engaged in the programming. Making customers full partners in developing new products can lead to new sources of innovative ideas and results that better meet their true needs.

Frito-Lay turned to customers to create an advertisement to run in the February 2007 Super Bowl, the most prominent and expensive television spot in advertising. The company invited consumers to submit their own ads in a competition, and vote on finalists, with the winner aired during the Super Bowl. It was a race that was compared to the popular television program *American Idol* (yet because the company chose the finalists, the process was not entirely in the hands of consumers).

Although the Frito-Lay ad was by far the most prominent user-generated advertisement aired on mainstream media, Converse, MasterCard, General Motors, Sony, and other companies have invited consumers to generate advertising. By inviting consumers, customers, developers and other partners to become active participants in the network, companies can increase engagement with their products and the success of new launches.

Why Disintermediation Didn't Happen: The Need for Thick Connections

In 1997, when B2B exchanges and other forms of B2B websites started to expand, speculation arose that companies such as Li & Fung would be cut out of the middle, or disintermediated. After all, there was a compelling argument that an agent who connects buyers with suppliers might be replaced by technology. Li & Fung realized that this could happen, however small the probability, and decided to move first. The company started its own online platform, initially for small to midsize businesses, called StudioDirect. StudioDirect gave small customers the platform to order products, essentially linking them with sourcing and supply chains electronically. The site offered users a set of product offerings that they could customize to meet their distinctive needs. Within these limitations, customers could connect through this platform to the factories in different parts of the world and draw through their own inventory.

> *Human relationships in business, as in most other things, are still paramount. The relationship Li & Fung seeks with its customers is narrow and deep.*

After only two years, Li & Fung shut down the business. The target market might not have been large enough to sustain it; however, it also shows the enduring importance of human relationships. Human relationships in business, as in most other things, are still paramount. Although some successful electronic exchanges have emerged, particularly where cost and efficiency are more important than relationships, even a commodity product, such as a polo shirt, has many variations in fabric, cut, and logos that have implications for how it is produced.

Building Narrow and Deep Relationships

Thick connections define the difference between an exchange and a network. An exchange, such as an online exchange, is a mile wide and a molecule deep. It can support many different transactions, but not relationships. Thick connections, in contrast, are narrow and deep. They are specific to companies and even staff. They allow loosely linked networks to operate by allowing formal and informal communication and coordination across the network, from suppliers to customers to end consumers.

The relationship Li & Fung seeks with its customers is narrow and deep. The relationship is not a "one contact point" relationship between Li & Fung and the customer's company, but a "multilevel" one—CEO to CEO, manager to manager, merchandiser to merchandiser, shipping clerk to shipping clerk. The ability at the top of the organization to pick up the phone and call the CEO of the client company or a supplier is crucial. These personal connections at every level of the organization hold the process together and also support solutions of complex problems.

Centering on the customer requires the right combination of loose coupling and tight information, thin operations and thick connections, value creation and supporting processes. The loose coupling of the organization allows for empowerment, customer focus, and entrepreneurship; tight information ensures that everyone is on the same page, that quality and production goals are met, and that deadlines are kept. This organization, illustrated in Figure 7-1, starts with the customer at the center and works out to entrepreneurial units, then to supply networks, and finally to the supporting infrastructure.

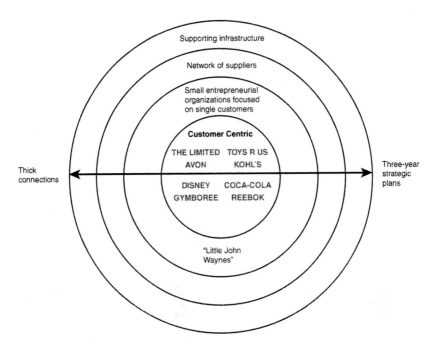

Thick connections

Three-year strategic plans

FIGURE 7-1   Organizing around the customer

Technology in the Service of the Business

Technology can serve an important role in building customer-centric organizations. In March 2002, Coca-Cola commissioned Li & Fung to design and build a customized extranet site. The site allows Coke executives and its many independent bottlers to order premium merchandise used to promote the brand. This meant that if a Coke branch office came up with a great promotion in one area, others might be able to order it for their regions. This can achieve economies of scale in production and also help individual offices of Coca-Cola reduce costs. It allowed Coca-Cola to spend more time and attention managing its soft drink business than its premium products. Integrated information technology can help ensure that the customer remains at the center.

Li & Fung is primarily an information company, and it has built extensive platforms for increasing transparency and linking the entire supply chain. The company was an early adopter of the Internet, setting up its first intranet in 1995 and first extranet in 1997. Li & Fung uses the technology to create thick connections across the entire supply chain for itself and other companies.

Technology can offer customers and suppliers a clear line of sight through the entire supply chain. Customers can send order information and track their orders throughout the online systems. Customers can see all the specifications for a project—when the fabric is delivered, when the cut and trim have been completed, and when the trim and buttons have been ordered.

As important as technology is, it needs to be placed in the service of the business, not the other way around. In applying technology, we have to think carefully about the interaction between the humans and the technology, and consider how the technology can serve the business. For example, as noted in Chapter 3, "Compete Network Against Network," during the SARS crisis, Li & Fung used videoconferencing to link to customers in Europe. Instead of relying on videoconferencing alone, the company sent executives to Europe, who sat down with customers there and used videoconferencing to connect back to managers in Hong Kong.

> *As important as technology is, it needs to be placed in the service of the business, not the other way around.*

Of course, as technology continues to develop, it will create new possibilities. If people on opposite sides of the world are able to converse through 3D holographic images in real time in more lifelike interactions, this could change how we use the technology. New collaborative platforms such as wikis (a website that allows users to add or edit content collectively) create opportunities to interact and build communities in different ways. Finally, a new generation of workers weaned on this technology might become increasingly comfortable interacting in new ways.

With Radio Frequency Identity (RFID) tags, connections become even more direct. At this point, the garments themselves have their own tags and can "talk" directly to the system; a human intermediary is not needed to track where they are in the process. This adds a level of transparency and precision to the entire process for suppliers and retailers.

Perhaps some day the machines will substitute for human intelligence, although we are still a long way from that point. (Although rule-based expert systems and other artificial intelligence approaches are advancing, human judgment is still critical at this stage.) The more important issue, however, is developing thick connections. These connections might become less personal and more technological in the future, but the important thing is that these connections are in service of the business. These connections hold together companies and their customers, always keeping customers at the center.

IT is, at best, a catalyst and an enabler; it is never an answer in itself. Just because an IT initiative can provide all the bells and whistles does not mean that the business wants or needs it, especially if it will take longer to get the product to market. Too often IT focuses on delivering one product or service, while the business or consumer is asking for another.

Because technology is in the service of the business, steps in the supply chain should be automated only when it makes business sense to do so. Li & Fung still retains and depends on human expertise at every crucial point in the supply chain. What is most remarkable about the Li & Fung technology is not the technology itself, but how important human judgment and experience continues to be. One might think that the complexity of global manufacturing—weighing deadlines, international exchange rates, shipping costs, and diverse options for manufacturing—would require a supercomputer to crank through a complex equation for optimization. Advanced management science tools are important in addressing the complex challenges of managing global networks, but the decisions are so complex that they cannot be entirely entrusted to machines. Skilled experts, supported by information systems, make decisions about where to manufacture and how to design each chain.

Only humans understand some nuances of the manufacturing process. For example, a red color from a certain source might bleed over everything. Chenille sweaters will be guaranteed to have trouble because they shed. A washed fabric, such as prewashed denim, is a complicated process that requires a judgment about the various shade of blue and the quality of the results. Only humans can decide.

People who have worked in manufacturing for a long time are like human search engines. For a pair of denim pants, they can rapidly narrow the best delivery, price point, source for the fabric, and where and how the wash should be done.

The world also changes very quickly: Even if one could write a computer program to embody the current complexity, it would be obsolete by the time it was complete. Consider the impact of civil disturbances in Bangladesh in May 2006. What should be the reaction? Should orders be pulled from factories there, or should companies wait and see whether the conditions will stabilize? Will it be temporary? (In this case, Li & Fung managers decided to wait and, in fact, were able to resume production.) This is a judgment call—and these types of decisions need to be made all the time. Computers can help, but at the end of the day, these decisions require a skilled manager who can use the technology in the service of the customer.

Customers Are the New Axis of the Flat World

The flat world might appear to be a world without an axis. Manufacturing processes can be moved to different countries or spread across multiple countries. Information can go from anywhere to anywhere. The true axis around which this world revolves could be the customer. The customer is the starting point for designing a supply chain or other business processes leading to the development and delivery of the desired products and services—the right product at the right place at the right time at the right price. The customer, whether a retailer or an end consumer, is the new center of gravity around which the supply chain is organized. The route through this world begins with a customer need and ends with a customer solution.

The route through this flat world begins with a customer need and ends with a customer solution.

Suppliers can be in any part of the world. Markets can be in any part of the world. Orchestrators can be anywhere. But the plumb line of this evolving and fluid network is a set of deep relationships and connections with customers. This is the axis around which the flat world revolves.

Are You Ready for the Flat World?

- How can you organize your business around customers?
- How would a customer-centric organization add value?
- What challenges for governance would it create?
- How can you build deeper relationships with your own customers?
- Where are more opportunities to add value for customers?
- How can you build thick connections with customers?
- How can you strengthen human connections?
- Does your technology serve the business, or does the business serve technology?
- Given the need to organize around customers, what do you need to do next?

8

Follow the 30/70 Rule to Create Loose-Tight Organizations

How do you keep outsourced partners engaged in your work without owning them? Set a target of having more than 30 percent of their business but not more than 70 percent. This provides focus and commitment but still allows for flexibility and learning.

Topper the Trick Terrier is a remarkable dog (see Figure 8-1). With voice-recognition software, the mechanical dog can respond to voice commands in English, Spanish, and other languages. This little pup talks, spins around, stands on his head, and does other tricks. Whereas many toys that do multiple tricks have complex systems of gears and pulleys to get all the limbs in the right place, little Topper uses a sophisticated set of motors and sensors that tell the integrated circuit exactly where his legs are positioned. And he retails for just $29.99.

FIGURE 8-1   Topper the global dog

Perhaps the most remarkable thing about Topper is how he was conceived, developed, and manufactured. Topper may not be a show dog, but he does have a global pedigree. His plastic parts come from Malaysia and Taiwan, his chips come from Taiwan, his stuffing comes from Korea, and his other parts are made in various locations in China. Topper is brought together by a company based outside Ghuanzou, called Qualiman Industrial Co Ltd. It has a combination of skills in electronics, plastic molding, and soft toys that are needed to create a hybrid product like Topper.

The development of Topper was the result of collaboration across organizations. The Original San Francisco Toymakers, Inc., in the United States, envisioned the toy and specified a set of features and a price point. The company worked with Li & Fung to develop and source the product. Li & Fung then turned to Qualiman, part of its network of thousands of suppliers. Engineers and product developers from the two companies worked with the San Francisco company to create Topper.

Li & Fung accounts for only about 25 to 30 percent of Qualiman's capacity. This is significant enough to be meaningful but small enough that Qualiman has flexibility and can also learn from interactions with other customers. With a workforce of more than 5,000 and sales of US$45 million in 2005, the manufacturer also works directly with some of the world's leading toymakers. This work has given the company broad capabilities and experience in trends and innovations in toy-making that it draws upon in working with Li & Fung.

Li & Fung and Qualiman have worked together for more than 10 years and have a trust and commitment that allows them to collaborate closely on design and production for Li & Fung's clients. For the first generation of Topper, the toymaker presented the conceptual design in January 2003. Li & Fung and Qualiman developed the first working model by March 2003. In April, with a few adjustments, they moved on to the final model, with fabric and material sourcing, chip development, and engineering development. This was completed just 12 weeks after the initial discussions. The first products shipped in July, and the company shipped 75,000 toys in the first year. Topper is a global toy that has resulted from a global collaboration.

Loose Coupling

With more networked systems, how do you get sufficient commitment from suppliers and other partners, yet still have sufficient flexibility to meet fluctuating demands? It is sometimes hard enough to get commitment from internal business units that are wholly owned and controlled. How do you get buy-in from partners who are not part of the organization?

Flexible networks depend upon loosely linked relationships; however suppliers need to be committed. But the network still has to have enough flexibility so the business can be reconfigured in response to customer demand. Li & Fung follows a 30/70 principle, the goal of which is to have more than 30 percent of the business of a given supplier, to be meaningful and ensure commitment, but no more than 70 percent of its capacity, to ensure flexibility and encourage learning.

> *Flexible networks depend upon loosely linked relationships. Li & Fung follows a 30/70 principle, the goal of which is to have more than 30 percent of the business of a given supplier, to be meaningful and ensure commitment, but no more than 70 percent of its capacity, to ensure flexibility and encourage learning.*

Think about the three states of matter—solid, liquid, and gas. The goal of loosely linked networks is a liquid state. A solid (commitment above 70 percent) is too inflexible to keep up with the changes of the modern world and shifting demands of customers. A gas (commitment below 30 percent) is too dispersed to be focused and productive. But this in-between liquid state has enough cohesion to get work done well, but enough flexibility to adapt to changing conditions.

In developing supply relationships, companies have to determine the right balance of control and flexibility. Companies need to actively assess how much flexibility and adaptability are needed for their specific market and product. Then they must determine the level of flexibility and commitment needed from suppliers. In a strictly transactional business—say, for an off-the-shelf commodity—it might not be necessary to have a minimum percentage of a supplier's output. But for a process partner, a strictly transactional relationship is rarely possible. Trust is essential. On the other hand, if commitment is more important than flexibility, it might argue for a tighter coupling with a supplier or even ownership. The looseness of the coupling needs to be adjusted to the market and environment.

Leveraging Learning

A fixed supply chain is a closed loop. Although it might promote efficiency improvements, it does not facilitate innovation. The goal is operational efficiency, not learning, which is often inefficient. The same players interact with one another, usually in the same way. This reinforces existing knowledge and perhaps leads to incremental improvements, learning how to do the current job better.

Interaction with other customers in other parts of the world gives suppliers a broader view of the context of their projects and a more creative solution set.

In contrast, the members of a 30/70 network work with many other clients besides Li & Fung. They learn about innovations in design and production from these interactions with other leaders from other parts of the world. They have a broader view of the context of their projects.

They are also developing their own innovative solutions to customer challenges. These solutions give them a larger and more creative solution set when it comes to addressing new challenges.

At the same time, interaction with Li & Fung gives these suppliers access to a broad pool of insights and best practices across many suppliers and customers. Suppliers can learn from these interactions even as Li & Fung learns from suppliers. The space in the 30/70 network creates room for creativity and learning.

Procter & Gamble also recognized the advantages of such loosely linked networks in driving innovation. Most companies rely upon internal research and development (R&D), which restricts innovation to inside the company and tends to lead to only incremental improvements. They try to bring new capabilities inside through acquisitions, alliances, and licensing. They also use skunk works projects (informal projects operating outside of formal processes) to spark innovation inside the organization. Facing declining innovation productivity inside the company, Procter & Gamble (P&G) turned the process inside out, pursuing a strategy of looking outside for innovation.

In addition to doing its own R&D, the company is focusing on what it calls C&D (Connect & Develop).[35] The idea of this "open innovation" is to identify and connect to innovations wherever they are in the world. P&G shifted from building on the work of 7,500 R&D people inside the company to joining these internal resources to 1.5 million people outside the company, with a permeable boundary between them. This has accelerated learning and led to the rapid introduction of innovations. Some 35 percent of its innovations have elements that have come from outside the company, from the Spinbrush to Swiffer. R&D productivity has increased by nearly 60 percent, and innovation success rate has nearly doubled.

Leveraging Capital

This dispersed network also allows for a capital-light strategy of leveraged growth. Loose coupling has allowed Li & Fung to expand its capacity and customer base rapidly without huge investments in factories and logistics. Li & Fung would need to invest an unimaginable sum of money to acquire the 8,300 suppliers in its network and the warehousing and logistics support needed to move products to customers.

Instead, using a capital-light strategy leverages the assets of other companies. Li & Fung acts as a knowledge broker, using its knowledge in sourcing to develop deep relationships with suppliers and manufacturers specializing in different stages of the production process, and leveraging its expertise to carry out the production of goods. Tapping into partners' assets also reduces risks involved in fixed assets and allows the company to flexibly respond to changes in markets and the business environment. This capital-light strategy also allows the company to enter markets more quickly and achieve substantial increases not only in sales, but also in profitability.

> *This dispersed network also allows for a capital-light strategy of leveraged growth.*

A capital-light strategy is associated with higher performance. A McKinsey study found that whereas the average Asian company needs $4 of assets to produce $1 of sales, the companies with the best performance needed only $1 in assets.[36] These companies used a capital-light strategy to improve their performance.

Benefits for Suppliers: Democratizing the Network

The benefits of loosely coupled networks for the network orchestrator and its customers were outlined in Chapter 3, "Compete Network Against Network" (including accessing best-in-world capabilities, increasing resilience, boosting speed, capitalizing on collaboration, and navigating global trade restrictions)—but what is in it for the suppliers? Is the network orchestrator merely shifting the risks and costs of the business to them? Many benefits arise from being part of the network.

Suppliers do shoulder more risk, in some cases, but not as much as it might appear. In fact, the risk might not be larger than the risk to an independent supplier from a customer going out of business or suffering a decline in demand. In some ways, the suppliers might have lower risks because they can benefit from the entire portfolio of work brought together by the orchestrator. If one client stops ordering, others take its place. In addition, the network provides other benefits to suppliers that are part of it, including:

> *Suppliers can realize many benefits in being part of the network, including benefits in aggregated demand, access to customers, access to knowledge, demand smoothing, and financing.*

- **Aggregated demand**—Li & Fung pools demand. It draws demand from large retailers and other customers, and divides it among several factories. By drawing together many small to midsize suppliers into a network, a small factory has access to a size of client that it could not serve on its own.

- **Access to customers**—Li & Fung's commitment to corporate social responsibility and reputation for quality might give a good factory without a long history or strong reputation access to clients it would not otherwise attract. Association with an established firm offers a "good housekeeping seal of approval."

- **Access to knowledge**—Li & Fung also offers suppliers the latest knowledge about processes, materials, and other areas so they can benefit from being part of the network. Li & Fung gives suppliers the opportunity to improve their performance and technology standards. Each of the company's product teams has established detailed and measurable benchmarks for suppliers, and staff closely monitors the performance level and the quality of products produced. The product teams give suppliers in-depth feedback regarding their performance, strengths, and weaknesses. The suppliers can work with the product teams to improve their shortcomings, and both parties can work toward bridging any performance gaps. This kind of mutual collaboration has created a powerful platform for continuous performance improvement. In this way, Li & Fung helps its suppliers climb the value ladder so they can better serve Li & Fung's clients at the higher end.

- **Demand smoothing**—As much as possible, given its large flow of projects, Li & Fung tries to keep good suppliers occupied. If an order from one client is cancelled, Li & Fung tries to bring another order from another part of the business into the factory. It is to Li & Fung's advantage to keep good suppliers active in the network, even though the two firms may have no formal long-term commitment.

- **Financing**—Procurement increases the factory's risk and up-front investment. After an order is confirmed with a customer, it could take months for a supplier to receive the letter of credit from the customer. The orchestrator can provide financing to some of its long-term suppliers, to lower their financing cost of, sourcing raw materials, for example. Because the orchestrator is managing the entire process, it has a better understanding of risks and can offer suppliers financing that an independent financial institution (which does not have this broader knowledge or control) could not provide. Unlike a bank, the orchestrator also benefits from improvements in the overall supply chain performance. If a manufacturer has relatively limited purchasing clout with its own suppliers, the orchestrator can leverage its supplier network to secure materials for that manufacturer at a better price and with a faster delivery date. This also helps smooth the supply chain and lower the total cost of production.

Overall, these benefits help to democratize the network. Individual suppliers retain their independence and autonomy but benefit from being part of this federation. By creating a market for the products and services of these small suppliers, the network orchestrator enables them to bid competitively on projects. Participation in this broader market should lead to the best possible price for their offerings. If certain manufacturing processes are becoming crowded and commoditized, the supplier can develop new capabilities that allow it to stand out, and the orchestrator can sometimes help in this process.

The more flexibility these suppliers have, the better they can redeploy their resources to receive the highest value. As part of the network, suppliers have greater autonomy and greater access to global opportunities. Production is no longer monopolized by huge vertically integrated companies.

Building and Expanding Relationships with Suppliers

To orchestrate and manage a global network of suppliers actively and effectively, companies must know their suppliers very well and develop cooperative rather than adversarial relationships with them. Orchestrators need to design and build their network and sustain the ecosystem of suppliers. Orchestrators need to balance empowerment with control and collaboration, respecting the flexibility and independence of members of the network, while aligning all players to achieve common goals.

The "network" is not a formally constituted entity. It consists of two important but intangible assets:

1. Deep knowledge of the manufacturing capabilities, special skills, business practices, and compliance standards, etc., of each country and supplier.

2. Long-term, cooperative relationships and trust with the suppliers.

Knowledge of Supplier Strengths

The network orchestrator needs familiarity with every aspect of each supplier in its network. This knowledge helps in assigning the right job to the right suppliers according to their respective strengths. For example, certain sweater suppliers are good at handling coarse wool and making bulkier sweaters in low gauges, but they might not be equipped with the best knowledge or machinery for ensuring the same quality and the same volume of throughputs for finer forms of wool and yarns such as angora or cashmere. This kind of intimate knowledge of suppliers, and the capability to coordinate and influence them, enables Li & Fung to put together a network of suppliers to satisfy orders from anywhere in the world.

Building the Capacity of the Network

The orchestrator needs to focus on building the overall capacity of the network, to keep suppliers engaged and ensure that the network has the capabilities needed for the future. As noted, the network orchestrator can help suppliers build and improve their capacities.

Suppliers with raw material sourcing and manufacturing problems can hardly turn to another supplier (basically, a competitor) for help and advice. But by working with clients and suppliers from all over the world, the orchestrator is in a better position to consolidate knowledge about market demands, production technology, capabilities and costs, latest design concepts, and product development, to share and help all the suppliers in its network. The orchestrator acts as the knowledge broker. It uses its knowledge in sourcing to develop deep relationships with suppliers and manufacturers that specialize in different stages of the production process, thus leveraging their expertise throughout the network.

Forging Connections to Suppliers

The orchestrator also needs to build the right connections with suppliers, to tie together a network that may not have fixed and formal relationships. Technology and other connections help tie together these loosely coupled networks. Whereas companies have focused on customer relationship management (CRM) at one end of the supply chain, they are also concentrating on improving supplier relationship management (SRM) on the other end. The goal of SRM is to make processes more effective and efficient between a company and its suppliers by creating common business practices and terminology. This improves processes for acquiring goods and services, managing inventory, and processing materials.

Improving connections with suppliers provides a richer flow of information from the factory floor to the rest of the organization. For example, if a problem arises in a factory in a remote part of the world, Li & Fung managers can patch in a global expert by video from Li & Fung headquarters to help solve the problem. Product inspection would typically be based upon the inspector's own observations or on samples sent with a long delay, but now these can be done (at least partly) through digital photos, videoconferencing, careful specification, and information streams from the factory.

A new system at Li & Fung called "road warrior" is putting the information in the hands of its staff working on the factory floor. An employee with a PDA on the shop floor can use a pen-based program (essential for dealing with character-based languages) to enter information that is then relayed to account managers at headquarters and even is accessible to the end customer. In the end, this creates an information chain right from the factory floor to the retail shelf.

Because communications infrastructures differ around the world, these connections need to be able to accommodate a wide range of suppliers. Li & Fung has systems that can operate with the most primitive or the most sophisticated technologies. The level of communication between country offices and the Hong Kong headquarters varies, depending on the sophistication of the country's telecommunication system. For instance, in more

> *Because communications infrastructures differ around the world, systems need to be designed to operate with the most primitive or the most sophisticated technologies.*

advanced markets, the local branch offices can be linked directly to Hong Kong. Staff at those offices can link up with the central databases and send digital photos of fabrics or products back and forth. In countries where telecommunication systems are relatively primitive, the branch offices use "thin connections." This could involve using Lotus Notes to communicate via e-mail and e-mail attachments, or even using phone and fax. Taken to the extreme, one could say that even if unsophisticated suppliers use telegraph, pigeons, or mirrors on mountaintops to convey production information, the basic system would still work effectively.

Loose but Not Laid-Back

Collaboration between customers, orchestrators and suppliers can create and manufacture innovative new products, such as Topper the Trick Terrier. But managing such relationships requires a delicate balance between loose and tight connections across the network.

Connections that are too tight become rigid, reducing flexibility and learning. Connections that are too loose become diffused, reducing focus and commitment.

The goal of loose-tight connections is to retain the freedom of both the company and its suppliers. Benefits emerge for the company, suppliers, and customers. This space allows for fluid adaptation and flexibility as the demands of customers and the constraints of the network change. But without rigid connections, the challenge is to develop systems to ensure the control and coordination of such networks. These networks need to be loose but not laid-back. By empowering the network, the orchestrator can design these networks and keep them humming—even improve their performance—without direct control. This begins with recognizing that you can have a well-functioning network without owning it.

Are You Ready for the Flat World?

- How loose or tight are your relationships with suppliers?
- What would happen to your relationship if you increased business with a minor supplier to 30 percent? What would happen if you reduced business with a major supplier to below 70 percent and added more suppliers?
- Given your markets and rivals, what is the ideal level of tightness of connection with suppliers? Should you have a 30/70 rule, or 20/50 rule, or some other?
- Beyond the percentage of work, what do you do to keep partners engaged and committed? What could you do?
- Given the need to build loose/tight relationships with partners, what do you need to do next?

Part III

Value Creation: Specialization and Integration

Companies need to balance building value through functional excellence and specialization within the firm, and building value through integration across the total supply chain and different functions within the firm.

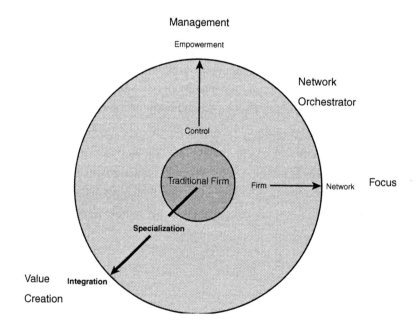

9

Capture the "Soft $3" by Looking Beyond the Factory

Although companies have focused on squeezing the last penny out of manufacturing, whole dollars are at stake in better managing the supply chain. A plush toy might cost $1 out of the factory door, yet it retails for $4. How can companies use better supply chain orchestration to capture this "soft $3"?

Manufacturing processes have improved dramatically in recent decades; now the biggest opportunities for cost improvements are often outside the factory. These opportunities come from looking across the supply chain, shifting from focusing on squeezing pennies from the "hard" manufacturing processes in the factory to recouping the "soft dollars" in the rest of the supply chain.

The opportunities beyond the factory are often several times as great as those inside. For example, a typical small plush toy that costs about $1 to produce by the time it rolls out of the factory might cost $4 at retail. The difference between the manufacturing costs and the final retail price is the "soft $3," as shown in Table 9-1. For garments or other products, this differential might be as high as a "soft $4 to $5," but the same general principle applies. More value or cost is added after the product leaves the factory than when it is inside.

> *A typical small plush toy that costs about $1 to produce by the time it rolls out of the factory might cost about $4 at retail. More value is added after the product leaves the factory than when it is inside.*

Not only is the total opportunity three or more times greater, but the factory costs have been squeezed and pushed and tweaked so much that it is very hard to extract another few cents out of the cost. Approaches such as Total Quality Management, Six Sigma, and automation swept through manufacturing and raised performance and efficiency. As best practices in manufacturing have spread, there are fewer opportunities for improvements inside the factory.

By looking across the entire supply chain, opportunities arise to realize the soft dollars through more efficient processes or by taking on greater responsibility for other parts of the chain. Previous chapters have contributed to optimizing this factory cost with dispersed manufacturing. This chapter deals with what further efficiencies we can achieve by working on the entire supply chain after the production process. This requires looking beyond the factory or center where the product or service offering is created to examine how value is created across the entire supply chain and the networks from which it is drawn.

TABLE 9-1   The Soft $3 for a Plush Toy

Component	Added Cost	Cumulative Total
Ex-Factory Manufacturing Cost		**1.00**
Inland Haulage and Consolidation Charge	0.08	
Freight and Insurance	0.11	
Defective Allowance, Variable Commission & Duty	0.24	
Warehousing and Distribution	0.12	
Financing (6 months at 10 percent)	0.05	
Tax	0.10	
Wholesale Profit After Tax	0.30	
Retail In-Store Cost of Goods		**2.00**
Retail IMU at 50 percent including:		
Markdown Reserve Net of Vendor Funding	0.40	
Shrinkage and Marketing Allowance	0.15	
Staff Cost	0.45	
Rental, Utilities, Equipment, Maintenance	0.40	
General, Administrative and Financing	0.30	
Tax	0.15	
Retail Profit after Tax	0.15	
Retail List Price		**4.00**

Opportunities to Capture the Soft Dollars

How can the "soft $3" be captured? Value is added or costs are incurred at every step of the supply chain between the end of the assembly line and the retail shelf, as illustrated in Figure 9-1. This $3 also might come from decisions in the factory or even in sourcing. For example, a factory that could execute orders on a fast turn could ensure product is in stock at the retailer and thus affect the value created in the broader chain. In the plush toy example shown in Table 9-1, the toy has a $4 list price, but might entail nearly $2 from in-store retail costs (including a small profit) and another $1 in costs of moving from factory to retail. Some 10 percent of the total $4 price goes to markdowns, usually due to a mismatch in supply and demand.

Better forecasting and processes to reduce these markdowns could be a significant opportunity for capturing more of this soft $3.

The cost of wholesalers, shipping, and logistics eats into the $3. Some of the "soft $3" goes to logistics such as taxes, duties, and handling charges, so improving these processes enables companies to capture more of these soft dollars. Although $4 is the retail price, the total could be larger as environmental concerns make retailers or manufacturers responsible for creating reverse supply chains to recycle or dispose of products after use. In this case, these additional dollars at the end of the chain offer opportunities for creating better processes and products that are easier to recycle or reuse. The costs at every step along the way can be reduced by taking an integrated view of the entire chain instead of focusing on one part. Among the ways to capture these soft dollars are boosting efficiency, improving coordination to reduce markdowns, creatively rethinking the chain, and taking on more of the chain. Let us consider each of these opportunities.

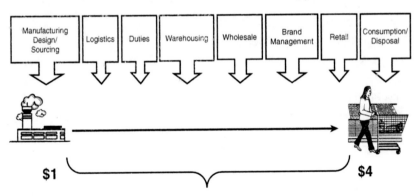

FIGURE 9-1   The concept of the "soft $3"

Boosting Efficiency: Containers and Flawless Execution

One way to capture these soft dollars is to simply make the extended supply chain work more efficiently. Standard-sized shipping containers were one of the best things to happen to modern logistics. The careful utilization of containers meant that shipments could be combined, lowering shipping costs and reducing overall logistics costs. The widespread use of containers in shipping led to modularization, more uniformity and better utilization of shipping capacity, resulting in big reductions in transportation costs. This is just one of the many ways that the supply chain has been streamlined and made more efficient. Time and money also have been shaved off the process of moving products across borders through electronic Customs clearance when the products are en route.

In taking on more of the supply chain, Li & Fung is moving from FOB ("Free on Board") arrangements, taking responsibility for the shipment only to the point of departure of the source country, to LDP (Landed Duty Paid), taking responsibility up to the shipment's arrival at the port and after the payment of duties in the customer's market. This means a greater responsibility for logistics, Customs clearance, and warehousing, as well as opportunities to capture more of these soft dollars.

Flawless execution also helps reduce costs of errors in the chain. Mistakes along the supply chain can be very costly for everyone involved. If a factory marks the bar codes on its cartons incorrectly, it can cost thousands of dollars because the wrong product is shipped to the wrong place. This adds to shipping costs and also means that retailers will not have the goods when they need them. The risks and costs of these mistakes are huge. Mistakes on the wholesale side can add up to more costs than the entire wholesale value of the product. Operations across the supply chain need to be flawless, and a key source of value is making these operations better, faster, and cheaper.

Improving Coordination: Minimizing Markdowns

As noted in Chapter 3, "Compete Network Against Network," improvements in the overall supply chain can increase responsiveness, helping to minimize markdowns and stockouts at retail. Markdowns are a flaw in the manufacturing process. Supply chain management is especially important in the apparel industry because the demand and price of a product are largely time-dependent. The suppliers and process steps for an apparel supply chain vary from season to season, from style to style, and even within the same style for the same season. The price of a garment starts declining as soon as the season begins, making the margins ever smaller.

> *Markdowns are a flaw in the manufacturing process.*

Concentration of retail power has also brought new attention to reducing markdowns, as suppliers are being asked to bear more of the burden of these costs. Retailers often seek "markdown money" from manufacturers, making them more responsible for failures to anticipate demand. This approach reflects the old adversarial view of the relationship between retailers and suppliers. Under the new cooperative supply chain model, it is better for everyone in the chain to create flexible responses to changes in demand. This means manufacturers should have an incentive to track and quickly respond to demand fluctuations. For example, customers in Li & Fung's private-label business allow Li & Fung to tap into the sell-through data at the retail store level. Managers in Hong Kong can see retail trends, anticipate demand, and either cut off poor products more quickly or plan for reorders for fast-selling merchandise. When a shirt sells or does not sell, this information ripples across the chain and back to the factories. This requires full collaboration of everyone in the supply chain for all parties to be linked.

In some cases, the cost of markdowns might exceed the entire cost of manufacturing. If the right product can be delivered more quickly to the shelves, this markdown can be reduced. This is why it is essential to achieve as fast a turnaround time as possible from order to delivery. Improvements can come from providing more transparency throughout the chain and allow more accurate forecasting of consumer preference and market demand. This more open process, in turn, can reduce cycle time by facilitating more timely decisions on postponement or speeding up manufacturing processes in response to market conditions.

Creatively Rethinking the Supply Chain

Value can also be created by improving product design and development on the front end of the supply chain or by creatively rethinking other stages of the chain. Whereas most plush toys are delivered fully formed, Build-A-Bear Workshop, Inc. (BBW), has created a thriving business by allowing its young customers to become active participants in manufacturing its toys. Children come to the stores and choose from among 30 or more unstuffed bears and other animals. The children can then select sound chips to place into the animal, with prerecorded audio or even their own personalized message. Then they fill the animal with a small satin heart and stuffing before the last stitch is closed. The animal is then groomed, named, dressed, and given a personalized birth certificate. The process is not merely manufacturing, but a customer experience that increases engagement.

Build-A-Bear Workshop, founded by entrepreneur Maxine Clark in 1997 in St. Louis, now has more than 270 stores in the United States, Canada, the United Kingdom, and Ireland, along with franchise stores in Europe, Asia, and Australia. The company had revenue of $437 million in 2006, an increase of more than 20 percent over the previous year. It achieved sales of $573 per square foot, which is excellent for a retail store but even better for a "factory" floor.[37] By involving the customers in the manufacturing and inviting customization, the company significantly increased the value of its product and the engagement of customers. It also ensured that customers would have exactly the right product they needed at the right time.

> *By involving the customers in the manufacturing and inviting customization, Build-A-Bear Workshop significantly increased the value of its product and the engagement of customers.*

Apple also creatively rethought the entire supply chain in music and entertainment with the introduction of the iPod and iTunes store to sell online music. Content might be seen as a concern outside the purview of an equipment and software company, but Apple recognized that it needed to take a broader view. This allowed it to create and capture more value by placing itself at the center of a network designed to deliver customized entertainment to individuals. More value lay in organizing and orchestrating these soft dollars than in manufacturing what otherwise might have been a generic digital music player, like many others on the market. The key was to look beyond the narrowly defined business to create value by focusing on the broader ecosystem.

Other companies have added value through customization. For example, Land's End began offering customers the ability to order jeans, men's dress shirts, and other garments tailored to their measurements. Even though these garments cost more, up to 40 percent of its customers choose customized garments, and a third reorder the personalized product. About a quarter of these customizers are new customers.[38] With this strategy, Land's End found a way to add $20 or more to the price of each garment, capturing additional value in the process while building its customer base.

> *By rethinking the supply chain and transforming the customer from a passive recipient to an active participant, companies have an opportunity to create and capture more soft dollar value.*

By rethinking the supply chain and transforming the customer from a passive recipient to an active participant, companies have an opportunity to create and capture more soft dollar value.

Taking on More of the Chain

In addition to improving the chain, companies can capture more of the soft dollars by taking on more of the chain. Li & Fung, for example, has extended its reach in the supply chain by establishing a significant onshore presence in the U.S. Through a series of strategic acquisitions and licensing arrangements, the company has added a full range of wholesale services that include product design, development, merchandising, marketing, logistics, distribution, and customer service located in its major market. The U.S. wholesale operation now has more than 600 employees, including 160 designers, and provides a full package of product offering from originating the idea, sourcing the product, replenishing inventories on core items and working closely with customer buying teams to develop private label, proprietary brands and national brand strategies.

By adding these front-end capabilities and leveraging historic strengths in managing the sourcing of products around the world, the U.S operation is able to operate at higher margins than the core business, while mitigating the risks by its involvement throughout the supply chain. This model has enabled the company to build a wholesale business with sales in excess of US$1 billion in a relatively short period of time and expand the company's customer base in the U.S. It has effectively captured a much greater share of the soft $3.

Higher Stakes

In a flat world of unpredictable demand, avoiding markdowns, stockouts, and expensive whipsaws in the supply chain is harder and more important. Fashion trends traverse the globe with the speed of an MTV program or YouTube video. Many new niches emerge or fade in this process. Capricious demand makes it harder to forecast. This raises the rewards of being quick and responsive.

> *In a flat world of unpredictable demand, avoiding markdowns, stockouts, and expensive whipsaws in the supply chain is harder and more important.*

Consumer markets are fragmenting into smaller segments. Price pressures are also intensifying. To keep prices at the same level, manufacturers and retailers have had to constantly reexamine and improve their processes. To address unpredictable demand, rapid cycle times, and retail pressure, companies need to focus more attention on what goes on outside the factory. Capturing the soft dollars means taking a broader view of the supply chain. It means orchestrating not merely the manufacturing process, but the entire chain.

Although the direct soft dollar value after manufacturing a plush toy might be $3, the intangible costs of a poorly designed or inefficient supply chain could be much higher. For example, while markdowns due to an excess of the wrong product are a critical concern, an even bigger problem could be lost sales, due to not having the right product in the store when customers arrive. How many customers walk into the store hoping to make a purchase, do not see what they are looking for, and then walk out again? Retailers rarely try to measure these lost sales. Because these customers have no contact with the retailer's cash registers and information systems, they are typically off the radar. In this case, the retailer might lose not only the immediate sale, but also future sales from the disappointed customer. (Catalog, online, and direct salespeople sometimes have a better read than physical retailers on lost sales as well as stockouts.) This is a significant cost to retailers, given the fixed costs of the store, marketing, and other expenses. And this is another opportunity to capture more of the ex-factory "soft dollars." Getting the supply chain right is crucial.

Many other companies can look at the "soft $3" in their industries. Former equipment companies such as IBM have recognized this opportunity as they have shifted more of their business to consulting. Although much of the equipment has become commoditized, offering little opportunity to profit on the equipment itself, high margins still exist in related consulting. Even service businesses might take a broader view of capturing value in their industries. Instead of leasing its experts to a company by the hour, a consulting company can use performance-based contracts that tie compensation to the ability of the consultant to help the client achieve its goals. The risks might be higher, but many more soft dollars are available from this approach than from transactional contracts based on billable hours.

The opportunities in a flat world often lie at the edges of the current business and mindset. The areas where everyone has focused attention probably offer scarcer opportunities for profit in a world in which best-practice knowledge travels rapidly. Seeing the broader opportunities requires a broader view of the entire chain.

Are You Ready for the Flat World?

- What are the broader opportunities for value creation in your own industry?
- What are the opportunities to address supply chain efficiencies beyond manufacturing or your core business (the "soft $3")?
- How can you capitalize on these opportunities to improve the supply chain?
- Can you take on more of the chain?
- What are the obstacles to capturing these soft dollars?
- Given the need to look for opportunities to capture the soft dollars in the network beyond your core business, what do you need to do next?

10

Sell to the Source by Bridging Marketing and Operations

The development of factories in emerging markets is often the precursor of the rapid growth of consumer markets. Sourcing from these markets can offer insights on selling to the same markets—if the knowledge of marketing and operations is brought together. How can you leverage your sourcing activities in emerging markets to build consumer businesses? How can you sell to the source?

During a market visit to the interior Chinese city of Chengdu in 2003, Gerard Raymond was struck by the emerging consumer market. The women passing on the streets were dressed in the latest fashions. There was a new department store being built. All the top brands were visible. It was a tangible shift in the wind. This city in Southwest China is located on the fertile Chengdu plain, known in Chinese as *Tianfu zhi guo,* translated as "the country of heaven" or "the land of abundance." But in the early part of the century, the city had not yet lived up to its name (at least in economic growth). Chengdu was located outside of the south and central districts where most of the market growth in mainland China was taking place. These latter districts accounted for the majority of the current business of Integrated

Distribution Services (IDS), the marketing and logistics and manufacturing arm of the Li & Fung Group. But from the market visit, it
was clear to Raymond, who leads IDS Marketing in China, that this
was about to change. Chengdu truly was becoming the land of abundance.

Based on these observations, Raymond expanded the company
office in Chengdu. The region grew from less than 1 percent of the
IDS Marketing business in China in 2004 to more than 10 percent in
a period of just 18 months. It underwent 286 percent growth from the
prior year, much faster than the overall Chinese market. Raymond's
on-the-ground insights helped the company recognize this opportunity early and get out in front of it. In emerging markets, rapid developments occur through the complex interaction of many factors, from
infrastructure building to changing regulations, to consumer shifts, to
the emergence of a few successful companies. You need to be close to
the ground to see them.

How can companies obtain such on-the-ground insights? For companies that are sourcing from China, India, or other emerging markets,
sometimes insights into emerging consumer markets come from the
floors of their own factories or call
centers (or those of network partners). But most companies are
siloed, so the knowledge from operations is not applied to marketing.
By taking a more integrated perspective of selling and sourcing in
emerging markets, companies can
capture deep knowledge of the
development of these markets that
they can use to sell to the source.

> *For companies that are
> sourcing from China,
> India, or other emerging
> markets, sometimes
> insights into emerging
> consumer markets come
> from the floors of their
> own factories or call
> centers.*

From Outsourcing Programming to Selling Generators in India

General Electric was a pioneer in setting up outsourcing centers in
India. This early involvement might have helped to lay the foundation
for a booming business in products to build the country's infrastructure.

The country's rapid economic growth is creating a tremendous demand for power generation, railroads, and other infrastructure improvements. Increases in consumer purchases of automobiles, electric appliances, and other products place new strains on the nation's ancient electricity grids, transportation systems, and other infrastructure. In 2006, GE sold $1.2 billion worth of generators, locomotives, and other products, more than double the previous year.[39] Its outsourcing operations give it a presence in the market that allows it to sell to the source.

IBM is expanding its outsourcing operations in India. This is partly to serve the global market, but also to meet the demands of a growing domestic market. Between 1992 and 2007, IBM reduced its U.S. staff by 31,000, while increasing its Indian staff by 52,000, in part to focus on domestic markets. As Michael J. Cannon-Brookes, Vice President for Business Development in India and China, told *The New York Times,* "India is at the epicenter of the flat world."[40] He went on to say that they can tap expert staff in India to serve clients both in the domestic marketplace and globally. They are selling to the source.

Microsoft is using its research centers in India to work on projects for the domestic market, such as software for users who are illiterate. Citibank has 22,000 employees in India and is expanding its staff in Asia, even as it has announced plans to eliminate or reassign 8 percent of its global workforce. India is not only a source of talent for Citibank; it is also the company's fastest-growing international market in terms of revenue.

Breaking Down Walls Between Marketing and Operations

Sourcing and selling, even with in the same organization, look at the world through different lenses. When companies think about selling globally, they usually think about shipping abroad. But if companies produce globally, they can also sell locally, using their insights from sourcing markets to build retail markets. The problem is that operations and service divisions specialize in sourcing, and marketing specializes in markets. Typically, these two worlds have only a few points of contact. Sometimes it is easier to link companies in Hong Kong and New York than to bring together different disciplines within a single organization. The world may be flat, but companies are not. To benefit from the synergies between the two sides of the business, they need to be linked.

There are many examples of the power of bridging the worlds of marketing and manufacturing. C&A, one of the leading fashion retailers in Europe, had long sourced from Latin America. Facing intense competition, the company withdrew from the market in 2001 and instead began focusing its attention on emerging U.K. markets.[41] C&A used its manufacturing base in Latin America to develop an extensive network of retail stores in countries such as Brazil, Argentina, and Mexico. In 1996, it opened its first five stores in Argentina and they expanded to Mexico in 1999, with plans to open 30 stores there by 2009.

Wal-Mart sourced from Mexico before establishing its retail operations there. In China, Wal-Mart is expanding its retail presence. By April 2007, the company had 72 supercenters, 3 Sam's Clubs, and 2 neighborhood markets in 40 Chinese cities. At the same time, more than 95 percent of the merchandise in Wal-Mart stores in China is sourced locally through 20,000 suppliers. Insights from its global sourcing could be valuable in developing the local retail business. Similarily, Tesco and Carrefour sourced from Eastern Europe before building retail operations there to serve the local market.

From sourcing, companies already know a lot about customers, the legal environment, and potential competition. Some of the potential customers in these markets are working on the floors of factories or managing them. Just as the "soft $3" took an integrated view of the entire supply chain, companies can find opportunities by taking a more integrated view of their own organizations. In markets that are evolving rapidly, marketing knowledge from sourcing can give early indications of emerging market regions such as Chengdu or unexpected threats such as slowing factory production that could lead to layoffs and a slow-down in the local economy. The primary focus of the network orchestrator might be on designing and managing networks to deliver products or services to customers in developed markets.

> *From sourcing, companies already know a lot about customers, the legal environment, and potential competition.*

But by taking a broader view—focusing on market development—companies can leverage their knowledge about the countries they are working in to sell to these same markets.

The flat world provides greater transparency and connection across cultures and time zones, but companies should not overlook the opportunities for increasing connections and transparency within their own firms. Developing an integrated strategy for selling and sourcing can contribute to economic development and build profitable businesses.

Opportunities in Emerging Markets

Emerging nations are the markets of the future. In 2003, Goldman Sachs pointed out in a landmark study that by the year 2050, the economies of Brazil, Russia, India, and China (BRIC) are expected to collectively eclipse those of the U.S., the U.K., Japan, Germany, France, and Italy.[42] Only the U.S. and Japan would be left among the richest six countries. To these original BRIC countries, some have added other markets, such as Mexico, South Africa, Eastern Europe, and Turkey. This growth will create rapid new consumer demand and changing spending patterns, leading to shifts in the demand for different types of products as these markets develop. Global companies need to be involved or will miss opportunities to grow with these economies.

The potential of this economic growth for the retail sector has already been demonstrated in China. Between 1979 and 2006, per-capita retail sales increased by 2,685 percent, from 185 yuan to 5,138 yuan. Between 2005 and 2010, the middle class (with incomes between US$7,230 and US$60,240) is expected to expand from 5 percent to 45 percent of households. Total retail sales of consumer goods hit 6.7 trillion yuan in 2005, posting double-digit growth since 2001. Retail sales are expected to reach 10 trillion yuan by 2010 and 20 trillion by 2020.[43] This is a tremendous opportunity for companies that can seize it. But competition is intense and the development of these markets is unpredictable, so realizing these opportunities is far from straightforward.

Markets Follow the Factories

Companies sourcing from emerging markets may already know their potential future customers. The workers, owners, and supporting businesses surrounding factories, outsourcing operations, and other enterprises of developing markets represent the beginning of the consumer market. The growth of manufacturing in emerging markets is helping to drive the development of consumer markets. Factory workers, many of whom have migrated from rural areas, have money in their pockets to spend for the first time. The factory managers and owners are looking at buying homes and cars. Service businesses around the factories are expanding. The emergence of consumer markets is a predictable outcome of the flourishing of industry and economic growth. Sourcing can offer a leading indicator of these developments. And asking export factories to sell to the local market can be a profitable way to meet the needs of these local markets.

The development of markets with manufacturing can be seen in coastal China. Much of the initial manufacturing sourcing in China was from the Pearl River Delta region, which is now one of the primary focal points for retail market growth. The development of manufacturing was a precursor to and driver of the development of service businesses and a flourishing consumer economy. But the thriving manufacturing business also led to higher salaries, which forced Pearl River factories to move to more sophisticated manufacturing. The workers who remained were typically better paid, boosting spending in the retail market.

The development of industry on the coast drove less sophisticated production processes inland within China, where costs were lower, or to other emerging countries. The completion of major highways in the eastern and central regions in 2005 extended China's supply chain network. This also meant that new sources of income arrived in these regions. In this way, the seeds of the next consumer growth markets were planted. By 2006, manufacturing was just moving to the far northern regions of China. This means it will be at least a couple of years before substantial retail business might be expected to develop. But develop it will. And by looking at the growth of sourcing, companies can identify opportunities for market growth.

Although Li & Fung has traditionally focused on the export supply chain business from China, tremendous opportunities exist in the import supply chain business to the Chinese market (and other emerging markets). Over the years, the company has mastered the export supply chain from the Chinese mainland and other parts of Asia. Now it can "flip" these skills and local knowledge, and apply them to import supply chains selling to consumers in China, Malaysia, Singapore, Korea, and other parts of Asia. Li & Fung has used its local insights to build retail businesses such as Circle K convenience stores and Toys "R" Us in China and other emerging markets. Whereas Li & Fung had sourced merchandise for Toys "R" Us, primarily from Asia, the company's Retailing Group now has built more than 49 Toys "R" Us outlets in China, Singapore, Malaysia, Thailand, the Philippines, and other areas. Li & Fung also established its first Circle K convenience store in 1985 and currently has more than 300 stores in Hong Kong, Macau, and an expanding presence in the mainland of China. In Korea, the company has outlets for Ferragamo, Mango, and GANT, and one of the leading convenience store chains. In Thailand, it has stores for Ferragamo, Calvin Klein Jeans, Country Road, GANT, and Billabong.

In some cases, the selling *precedes* sourcing. The development of local markets requires manufacturing closer to the markets. For example, Brazilian-based Marcopolo became one of the world's leading bus manufacturers by expanding into emerging markets. It began exporting in 1961 and is now present in more than 100 countries. After moving into Portugal, it established a presence in Argentina in 1997, then Mexico in 1999, and South Africa in 2001. It has succeeded by building local manufacturing sites and tailoring products based on a deep understanding of local culture and market needs. This is another route to market development, but even here, sourcing operations can benefit from the insights from marketing if the two sides collaborate.

Seizing Opportunities While Avoiding Ghost Malls

One challenge in emerging markets is not to arrive too soon or too late. Hundreds of shopping malls have been built in China since the start of the new millennium, in anticipation of the nation's growing prosperity and emerging middle class. Many of these malls were filled with upscale goods. But some of the growth was too far ahead of the curve, creating what have been dubbed *gouwu zhongzin* (ghost malls).[44] The upscale Superbrand Mall in Shanghai's Pudong suburb was languishing with 45 percent occupancy in 2004, until it was reinvented as a working-class "rice-and-noodles mall," increasing occupancy to 95 percent. A market that may not be ready for Gucci could still present "rice-and-noodles" opportunities.

Timing is everything in emerging markets. The challenge is to ride the wave of consumer market growth without getting too far ahead or behind. Many risks and perils could slow the process of market development. Hiccups in growth arise. Even a temporary slowdown could be devastating for businesses that have had to make large investments to succeed. Companies need to have their fingers on the pulse of these markets.

> *The challenge is to ride the wave of consumer market growth without getting too far ahead or behind.*

With more than a billion consumers, it appears clear that China will someday become one of the most important consumer markets in the world. But how and when this market unfolds is much less certain. The trajectory of this growth is often quite complex. The country faces economic, medical, social, and infrastructure challenges. Growth often moves in fits and starts, affected by internal policies and external shocks. As in Chengdu, unexpected hot spots can emerge suddenly. Sourcing can help avoid the ghost mall syndrome and offer insights into many drivers of market development, including regulations and policy, risks, competition, detailed market information, and market shifts, as examined next.

> *Sourcing can offer insights into many drivers of market development, including regulations and policy, risks, competition, detailed market information, and market shifts.*

Regulations and Policy

Government policies directly affect growth in emerging markets, and sourcing can provide insights on how these regulations are changing. For example, China's Eleventh Five-Year Program (2006–2010) included initiatives that will have a significant impact on rural market development by promoting market growth outside of the largest cities. The plan calls for the construction of a "new socialist country-side." In February 2005, the government launched a project to improve rural retail infrastructure, the "Market Project of Thousands of Villages and Townships." The goal was to create a rural retail network covering 70 percent of villages within three years. The initiative has encouraged major supermarkets and other chains to expand their presence in the countryside. The majority of the more than 6,000 stores of new Chinese retailer Cooperation Joint-Stock Trade Chain Co. Ltd are located in the countryside. The Sunong Group now has nearly half its 1,600 stores in the countryside.

The Chinese government also has sponsored initiatives to boost consumption in a nation where consumers still save nearly 40 percent of their incomes, using tax policy, free education, and agricultural protections. The government has launched initiatives to expand credit card use, an intervention that will affect the spending patterns and retail development across the country.

Sourcing from a region requires understanding local laws and political leadership. These insights are critical in building a business to serve these markets. In addition, sourcing provides an understanding of regulations (although they are not always the same for imports and exports) and the policy discussions that will shape the future business environment.

Contributions to a country's trade through exports also gives companies a more favorable position in developing an import business. Many countries want to attract foreign exchange so that a company exporting goods from those countries might enjoy more favorable treatment for import activities. One of the direct benefits of selling to the source is that companies can use the goodwill and foreign exchange generated by exports to ask for better licenses to import, especially in developing countries.

Risks

Sourcing can offer insights into the risks of specific markets. The Opacity Index, for example, identifies 65 variables related to risks in different countries around the world. The index is a rigorous tool for assessing the relative risks of foreign markets, allowing managers to weigh and compare diverse forms of risk from sources such as unclear legal systems, regulations, economic policies, corporate governance, and corruption.

A sourcing operation can provide similar, more finely tuned, real-time insights into risks in specific cities or regions. It can provide an early-warning system for changes that might increase or decrease these risks.

Knowledge of Competition

A market presence helps to understand the competitive environment. With growth, the retail sector in China has become more sophisticated, modernized, and competitive. Although foreign companies have been very active in the Chinese market, intensely competitive local players have continued to lead wholesale and retail businesses. According to statistics released by the Ministry of Commerce and the China Chain Store and Franchise Association, sales revenue of China's top 100 chain stores increased 25 percent in 2006 over the prior year. The top 100 chain stores operated 69,100 outlets in the country, employing 2.04 million people, up 31 percent from the year before. To understand these local players, companies need a deep knowledge of local rivals, which sourcing can offer.

Detailed Local Market Knowledge

Local tailoring is essential for success in local emerging markets. For example, home improvement retailer B&Q realized that there is a much more limited do-it-yourself market in China than in Western markets and has provided one-stop shopping, including tool repair, timber cutting, paint mixing, and installation services. Starbucks, recognizing that Chinese customers prefer to stay in the store, has added more seating and a menu to its stores in China. It even offers its own Starbucks' moon cake. Specific cities and regions require more precise tailoring, including understanding of local culture and dialects and other idiosyncrasies of these markets. This tailoring requires deep market insights that can be gained partly through sourcing.

As with many emerging markets, China is not a single market, but a collection of local markets. These markets differ based on income, consumer behavior, tastes, climate, infrastructure development, language, culture, and other dimensions. Sourcing can offer insights into the regions with the greatest growth potential. Whereas urban areas in China are growing wealthy, millions of rural households are living in extreme poverty. The National Bureau of Statistics (NBS) estimates that the consumption level of these rural residents is about a decade behind that of their urban peers. Chinese markets are very fragmented, with most of the growth concentrated in the Eastern coastal regions, particularly in the Pearl River Delta (including Guangzhou and Shenzhen), the Yangtze River Delta (including Shanghai), and the Beijing-Tianjin-Hebei regions. Guangdong province alone, with consumer retail sales of more than 911 billion yuan in 2006, accounted for nearly 12 percent of China's total retail sales. On the other hand, Guizhou's per-capita retail sales were comparatively anemic—less than a quarter of Guangdong's and less than a tenth of Beijing's. Many of these regions are active centers for sourcing, so a presence in these areas can offer insights on different rates market growth.

Market Shifts

With rapid growth, emerging markets are constantly changing. Sourcing operations can offer insights into the speed and direction of these changes. As top-tier cities in China become more saturated, the battlefield has shifted to second- and third-tier cities such as Chengdu, Tianjin, Quingdao, Shenyang, and Nanjing. Mergers and acquisitions have resulted in rapid growth and consolidation of the retail industry.

There are predictable shifts in consumption as markets mature. Consumers become more aware and discerning. They spend more on durable goods and services. They spend on education and self-improvement, dining, housing, telecommunications, and travel. As incomes rise and life becomes more hectic, time-starved consumers demand greater convenience. They are also more conscious of the environment. Marketers need to watch for these shifts in spending patterns and shape their initiatives to the stage of market development.

In identifying future markets, companies need to look upon their elite tier of customers—the business owners and managers—who might form the initial market. But they also need to look beyond these high-income segments. In the past, companies might have been able to apply the 80/20 rule, focusing on the 20 percent of customers that contribute 80 percent of profits. But in intensely competitive markets, they cannot afford to overlook the other 80 percent of the market. In developing and emerging markets, this 80 percent includes the factory workers. This segment might be a small part of revenue today but could be the core market of the future as incomes continue to rise.

Whereas most of the initial sales of Li & Fung's Circle K convenience stores were in the sophisticated urban markets of Hong Kong, accounting for some 250 stores, the future is in less wealthy mainland Chinese markets. The company is expanding rapidly into mainland China, having added some 50 stores by 2006. Some of these stores are investments in the future. Companies need to begin building a network in more rural areas that will be ready in five or ten years when the market is more fully developed. These long lead times in building operations and reputation require a solid understanding of where these markets are today and where they are headed, insights that the sourcing business can provide.

Although a presence in smaller cities and rural areas requires a detailed understanding of these markets and the capability to read early signs of market development, it can give companies a jump on competitors in these regions. These smaller markets also can present opportunities for testing new concepts without the risks of experimenting in expensive and highly competitive urban markets. Such an outside-in strategy can be used to establish new concepts or brands in a less crowded market and then, if successful, can help in moving into larger cities.

For example, Li & Fung helped a European firm set up one of the first high-end spas in Chengdu. This new entrant might have been lost among many offerings in Shanghai, but it stood out as a gem in the local market. Real estate and other costs were also much lower.

If successful, the concept and brand can be moved into urban markets later. However, this strategy works only if the same or similar segments exist in both locations. These smaller markets serve as a laboratory for new product and brand development. A broad presence in a country such as China, particularly in secondary or tertiary markets, allows for this type of experimentation.

Bringing Worlds Together

The story of selling to the source is not always as neat as it sounds. One might think that consumers will stand at the end of factories in China with their hands outstretched and receive the goods for their domestic markets. Not in today's world of regulations and taxation systems. Because export production receives special tax breaks, manufacturers are sometimes reluctant to sell to their home markets, for fear it will expose them to taxes on their much larger export sales as well.

Regulations and tax structures have led to circuitous twists in the supply chain in these developing markets. For example, many of the toys made in Chinese factories for the Toys "R" Us stores in China are first exported to Hong Kong. They are then reimported to China, at a substantial cost. It might not seem to make sense for a stuffed bear to travel from a factory in Shanghai to Hong Kong and then back to a retail store within a few miles of the original factory. But such convoluted paths are a reality in our modern world. Although the world is becoming flat, global trade regulations are still as lumpy as the surface of the moon, as we will consider in Chapter 11, "Policy: Building a Borderless Business in a World of Nation-States." But even in these cases, sourcing insights can alert companies to regulations and restrictions that might affect their selling businesses.

These regulatory mazes are often not the most significant barrier to selling to the source. Often, one of the most substantial barriers is the fiefdoms that exist in most large organizations. By bridging these silos and connecting different parts of the business, sourcing operations can offer a window on selling to emerging markets. This creates a virtuous cycle, with the growth of sourcing contributing to the development of retail markets. The more the sourcing operations expand in a specific country or region, the more money consumers will have to spend on products and services. The more consumers spend, the more new businesses are attracted to the region and the more the economy grows. Sourcing and selling are integrally linked in developing markets. Companies need to be sure to create connections between operations and marketing and other functional areas of their own companies so that they can seize the opportunities and manage the risks of selling to the source.

Are You Ready for the Flat World?

- What opportunities do your sourcing operations create for developing businesses to sell to emerging markets?
- Where are your next big market opportunities emerging? How can you take advantage of them?
- How can you gauge the timing of the development of emerging consumer markets to avoid getting too far ahead of the curve?
- What are the obstacles to bridging functional silos in your organization?
- Given the need to bridge silos and sell to the source, what do you need to do next?

Part IV

Implications for Policy and Practice

The emerging flat world has implications for policymakers and managers who have to operate in this world.

11

Policy: Building a Borderless Business in a World of Nation-States

The modern supply chain is a high-performance machine that can move with efficiency and precision that are unprecedented. But the regulations that govern this world create mountain ranges that slow the progress of supply chain improvements, or localized tunnels and superhighways that benefit certain regions. How does policy need to change in the flat world? What do business leaders need to know about policy to navigate this lumpy and shifting terrain?

Li & Fung once was sourcing jackets from a factory in an emerging market during a period of severe economic crisis and starvation. The company had arranged payment through a bank letter of credit for the factory. Then managers in Hong Kong received an e-mail from the factory managers. They asked Li & Fung to withdraw the letter of credit. They were not interested in money. In this environment, money was worthless because there was no food to purchase. The factory managers sent instead a list of food and daily necessities—mostly rice, flour, and canned goods—that they wanted instead of the funds. The food was sent down in the shipping container and emptied out, and the garments were shipped back. The factory managers were concerned with keeping their employees and their families from starving. International trade literally kept them alive.

Trade policy might sometimes seem like an abstract concept, but global trade has a real impact on the lives of many people and the economic progress of nations. As in this case, it can even have life-and-death implications. Unfortunately, as was the case with the starving factory workers, political and economic interests often lead to suboptimal outcomes. Parochial concerns take priority over the practical business activity of understanding customer demand, meeting it with the best and lowest-price products possible, and creating value in the process.

The primary concern facing business leaders in the flat world is how to design the best possible supply chain and the best possible network, to deliver the best product at the best price. But this work is complicated by complex and layered regulations and restrictions. These distortions that shape the business terrain have a tremendous impact on the networks and chains that are possible for businesses to create. Business leaders, particularly those engaged in network orchestration, need to understand this shifting terrain and the forces that shape it.

New Silk Roads

On a topographical map of China spread out on a conference table in Li & Fung's Hong Kong office, the wisdom of the old Silk Road is clearly visible. This classic trade route from China was bound by physical geography. Camels and horses carried silk, porcelain, and other goods through winding valleys, through mountain passes, and from oasis to oasis across vast deserts to the west. Hong Kong itself owes its position as a global trading hub largely to its geographic position as the best deepwater port in Southern China. In the old days, the Silk Road represented the best route through a world of great distances and very difficult logistics. In this world, geography was destiny.

Today the basic challenge of trading, or engaging in any other global business activity, is the same—linking products to customers. Where can companies find the best products in the world? How can the right products be delivered to customers at the right time and at the right price? What are the best routes through this world? The paths through this world are more fluid. Although the Hong Kong port continues to deliver the majority of goods from the Pearl River Delta of China to the world, an increasing percentage of goods (now 34 percent by value) is traveling by air. A port needs to be built on a coast, but an airport can be built almost anywhere. Even the vast distances that separate factories in Asia from retail stores in North America or Europe are now less significant. Information flows instantly. Goods flow quickly. The physical mountains and valleys are less important. Geography is no longer destiny.

Regulatory Mountains and Superhighways

While physical terrain is less significant, other constraints—particularly regulations—are shaping the new global business terrain. Regulation and trade agreements sometimes create mountains that block trade (through quotas, safeguards, or other constraints). Regulations and trade arrangements can also build tunnels or superhighways (through preferential bilateral agreements between two countries) that facilitate trade (see Table 11-1 for examples). The result is a patchwork of shifting multilateral, bilateral, and local regulations. Just as traders in the past needed to understand the Silk Road, business leaders need to understand these new Silk Roads and the forces that shape them.

TABLE 11-1: Mountains and Superhighways

Some bilateral trade agreements create new mountains, while others create superhighways between specific countries. Consider a few examples.

Mountains	Superhighways
Antidumping restrictions and safeguards imposed on Chinese exports (e.g., European anti-dumping tax on Chinese shoes or U.S. measures against Chinese paper exports)	NAFTA: the U.S., Canada, and Mexico
Import license for imported goods from China in Mexico and Brazil	Qualifying Industrial Zone (QIZ) bilateral agreement of the U.S., Israel, Egypt, and Jordan, allowing duty-free access to the U.S. market
Antisurge mechanisms of the WTO that reimposed a quota system on textile exports from China even after the quota system ended for the rest of the world in 2005	2007 Korean-U.S. Free Trade Agreement (KORUS FTA) between the U.S. and South Korea

Global trade quotas and safeguards mean that it is sometimes advantageous for products to zigzag across borders on their way to completion. For example, although it might make economic sense to produce a garment entirely in Zhuhai in southern China, regulations take the garment on the journey from Zhuhai to Macau and back again. The fabric is dyed and cut in Zhuhai, transported to Macau for "major assembly" (sewing on the arms of a shirt, for example) that qualifies Macau as the country of origin for the garment. The shift then comes back to Zhuhai for finish work, embroidery, washing, pressing, pricing, and packaging before returning briefly to Macau for Customs clearing. It is a long and winding road that makes sense only in the light of a Byzantine maze of regulatory hurdles.

> *Whereas physical mountain ranges evolved only over millennia, the new regulatory and political mountains and tunnels of the modern world can change in months or days.*

The new Silk Roads of global business are much less permanent than past trade routes. Whereas physical mountain ranges evolved only over millennia, the new regulatory and political mountains and tunnels of the modern world can change in months or days. This means that the road that offered a clear path one day could be closed the next, with a new road appearing elsewhere in its place. The old Silk Road endured for generations, but the new Silk Roads can be reconfigured overnight.

Because trade agreements can change rapidly, businesses have to continuously monitor and adjust to the changing conditions. This raises the cost of production, a price that consumers ultimately pay—often the same consumers whose jobs the regulations are ostensibly trying to protect.

Increasing Complexity and Bilateral Agreements

Not only is the new geography complex, but it also is often much harder to chart, particularly in an age of bilateral agreements. Formal quotas and high tariffs were once the most prominent feature of global trade barriers. Now, although formal quotas and high tariffs have been reduced or eliminated, the current global playing field is shaped in more subtle and piecemeal ways. Trade is facilitated or slowed by a web of ad hoc bilateral agreements between separate countries. Quotas have been removed, but safeguard measures still are designed to prevent a country such as China from "damaging" the industries of other WTO members. The rise of trading blocs such as NAFTA in North America and the European Union also has created distortions in the flat world. In contrast to multilateral agreements that create a more clear and level playing field for all, these bilateral agreements and safeguards add to the lumpiness and the fog of the flat world. Bilateralism distorts the flow of goods, throws up barriers, creates friction, reduces flexibility, and raises prices.

> *A web of ad hoc bilateral agreements between separate countries is shaping the global playing field in more subtle ways.*

Most of these bilateral agreements are not motivated by sound economic thinking; instead, agreements are forged primarily for political purposes. The United States rewards allies such as Egypt with favorable trade agreements that, in effect, create a smooth superhighway between the two countries while leaving other countries behind on the off-ramps. On the other hand, trade restrictions that create mountains target certain countries, primarily as sanctions for political, military, or economic actions.

The complexity of these crisscrossing bilateral agreements, with no central design, has led to what trade experts call "the spaghetti bowl effect." Companies incur huge costs and have a hard time just keeping track of all these regulations. For small firms, it is nearly impossible. Bilateral agreements cause business to suboptimize. A company might design the best supply chain in the world, but then it needs to be modified to navigate through the maze of bilateral agreements and other restrictions.

No perfect market exists. Some friction will always appear, and in a world of global organizations and national regulations, many lumps will arise in the flat world. We should avoid making the mistake of those theoreticians in financial markets who adhere to the perfect market theory. They failed to recognize that these are very human systems and decisions at work that have a very significant influence on the markets. We are dealing with a world that is not completely flat.

Advantages of Nations

Network orchestration challenges traditional thinking about the advantages of companies and nations. Economist David Ricardo's seminal work proposed that the competitive advantage of a nation is based on specialized resources that are imperfectly mobile (sticky) and not easily imitated. But the flat world makes knowledge and other resources increasingly mobile and more easily imitated. Specialization is still important, but integration becomes more central to creating advantages and value. As with businesses, the capabilities a nation owns are not necessarily as important as the capabilities it can *connect to*. This has implications for policies that are designed to protect or preserve advantages of specific nations.

If advantage goes to the integrator, is the Ricardian law of competitive advantage repealed in the flat world? For now, this is somewhat of a hypothetical question. A web of national regulations in a global economy represents a countervailing force working against the flattening of the world. As economist Pietra Rivoli points out in her journey through the global garment industry described in *The Travels of a T-Shirt in the*

Global Economy, the global garment industry is not a free market: From the subsidized cotton grown in Texas fields to the garment factories in China, the chain is driven more by regulation than by market forces. "It is political reactions to markets, political protection from markets, and political involvement in markets, rather than competition in markets, that are the center of my T-shirt's life story," Rivoli writes.[45] Perhaps the only true market is at the end of the line, she notes, in sales of used T-shirts to developing countries.

> *Political forces are working determinedly to keep the world lumpy, establishing new mountain ranges and building tunnels and superhighways for favored trading partners.*

Democratization of Trade

As any investor knows, market inefficiencies create opportunities. A network orchestrator such as Li & Fung, with flexible global networks, is actually well positioned to take advantage of the shifting borders of a world of bilateral agreements. With a strong global network of suppliers, the orchestrator has an advantage in responding to unpredictable changes in regulations. But as with the absence of free markets, the absence of a truly flat world adds to the complexity and inefficiency of global business overall. Everyone wins in the long run the more the world is made flat.

A truly flat world leads to a democratization of trade. Each country or company can contribute according to its skills and capabilities, to develop its own competitive advantages. This democratization means that small firms with limited capital can succeed as part of a broader network. Globalization has tremendous value for the countries and companies that participate, but the shape of the global playing field affects the depth and distribution of these benefits. Multilateralism creates value and democratizes the global economy. Everyone has a place. The bilateral systems create oligarchies that discriminate, putting everyone in their place. Although they might create opportunities in the short term for companies that can navigate around these obstacles, overall they lead to suboptimal supply chains. In the end, this hurts everyone.

Businesses should not have to design systems to qualify under "rules of origin" to obtain preferential treatment. Instead, the question should be, "What is the optimal way to deliver the best product to the right customer at the right time at the right price?" That is the only thing network orchestrators should be worried about. Why should they worry about the point of "substantive transformation"? Decisions should be made on the basis of economics alone. For the future world-trading regime to mirror economic reality and to allow the use of modern business strategies, we need a single overarching multilateral framework for trade. We can have either a flat world or a patchwork of crisscrossing mountain ranges and tunnels.

Policymakers need to take a careful look at the impact and implications of bilateralism, and business leaders need to urge them to do so. A multilateral world trade system is our very best hope for addressing the broad range of issues such as market access, tariff and nontariff barriers to trade, trade in services, and trade facilitation. With respect to market access and tariffs, multilateral solutions will help us optimize the efficiency of the complex cross-border flows generated by dispersed manufacturing.

The world is filled with borders, and all of them are guarded and controlled. Businesses need to navigate through or around these restrictions and change themselves as the rules change. Although great strides have been made in the liberalization of trade policy, one of the greatest obstacles to fulfilling the potential of network orchestration and harnessing the flat world is a political and economic environment that is not aligned with this new model. These systems tend to protect mediocrity and increase costs.

Deciding Where to Play

The flat, networked world creates opportunities for countries to create finely tuned strategies for where to play. Whereas countries once looked at developing whole industries—such as automobiles and semiconductors—in a networked world, they can work with businesses to make decisions about what processes they can best contribute to global supply chains. In Thailand, for example, the government encouraged the Thai auto industry to look for the niches in the global supply chain where it could add the most value. Now all of Thailand is talking about the global supply chain and which process in the chain Thailand should focus on. Thailand is looking at ways to tie its strengths into global supply chains. In a connected world, countries are increasingly making decisions about a specific vision or strategy for where to compete in that world. Will the country become a hub for manufacturing, as China has, or will it become a financial center, as in Dubai?

To support these decisions about where to play, governments can invest in research, education and other areas to strengthen specific capabilities. With China's accession into the WTO, the increase in foreign investments is expected to generate many market opportunities. These will further encourage both local and foreign enterprises to source from the Chinese mainland. Some regional clusters have already been developed in industries such as personal computers and electrical appliances. These clusters encompass a wide array of vertical and horizontal linkages so that components such as compressors and chips can be produced in China.

Governments also can support dynamic and flexible organizational structures and initiatives. Pilot schemes such as granting share options or employee shares in China are a step in this direction. These incentive schemes can link the compensation of management and employees with their overall performance and the future development of the enterprise. In this case, employees can focus on growing their companies' long-term value instead of solely concentrating on short-term returns. Finally, government leaders can encourage the improvement of product quality and application of technologies, and provide education to ensure that they have skilled workers.

Country of Origin: The Need for a New Language

Even the language of global trade is designed for a different world. The supply chains that have emerged in this flat world defy simple methods of categorizing trade. Whereas regulations and analysis are based at the country level, business is global. Consider the concept of "country of origin." What does this mean when a product is produced across many countries? Does a sweater become a sweater when the sheep is sheared? When the yarn is spun? When the yarn is knitted to shape? When it is dyed? When the sweater panels are linked? When the last button is sewn on? These stages might occur in many different countries, so the concept of "country of origin" becomes quite problematic. Because the last processes usually (but not always) define the country of origin of a product, and China is often at the end of this dispersed manufacturing process, it has a huge trade surplus with the U.S. and other parts of the world, while every one of the ten ASEAN countries supplying parts in this process has a growing trade surplus with China. Different importing countries often have different rules of origin, generally based on where "substantive transformation" occurs (such as sewing the sleeves on a shirt rather than the buttons).

As we shift our focus from competition between companies to dispersed supply networks that compete network against network, we need to change the way we look at and regulate this world. Concepts such as "substantive transformation" and "country of origin" need to be reexamined. We need new language to reflect the realities of dispersed manufacturing.

Ferraris on Dirt Roads

Modern supply chains and logistics have become tremendously efficient. In the ideal, they are like finely tuned Ferraris racing along the straight and open autobahns of the flat world. On these straight and flat roads, they can go faster and do more than supply chains of the past. But in actuality, these Ferraris are forced to drive on dirt roads and cross mountain ranges with few tunnels and passes.

Trade networks are helping to stimulate local economies and contribute to education and health. They can be a stabilizing force between countries engaged in commerce. (Thomas Friedman had proposed the "Golden Arches Theory of Conflict Prevention" that no country with a middle class large enough to support a network of McDonald's would declare war against another McDonald's country. He updated this to the Dell Theory, that no two countries that are part of the same major global supply chain, such as Dell's, would go to war.)

Although concerns arise about the impact of shifts in manufacturing in "hollowing out" various industries (as domestic industries move abroad), this has been a continuous process. China has built up tremendous production capabilities in labor-intensive consumer goods industries, but it has a crying need for raw materials and intermediate components. Best-in-class production in these labor-intensive areas might migrate to other regions such as Bangladesh or Vietnam, and the existing regions will have to develop new competencies. Ultimately, China's own garment industry might be "hollowed out" by emerging nations in Asia, Latin America, Africa, or other parts of the world.

For business leaders, the debate over hollowing out can be a distraction from developing products and supply chains that deliver the most value. Remember the days when U.S. legislators were smashing Sony radios or raising the alarm as semiconductors migrated to Taiwan. These issues grabbed the headlines but only delayed economic progress. Intel did not go out of business, but moved in very profitable new directions with the rise of the personal computer. Although Sony became a powerhouse in consumer electronics with its Walkman, this did not stop U.S.-based Apple from surging back with the iPod. To the extent that free markets exist, the best product wins, no matter where it comes from. Competition in the global market today is not a zero-sum game.

While it might not always have life-and-death implications, as in the story that opened this chapter, global trade regulations affect every one of us. There is something in it for everyone: knowledge-intensive jobs, manufacturing jobs, jobs creating components and inputs, and service-related jobs. The multilateral system enables each location around the world to contribute according to its skills and capabilities, and to develop its own competitive advantages. Modern production systems are multilateral, not bilateral. Our trade regulations also need to be multilateral. Multilateralism democratizes the global economy. Like a finely tuned Ferrari, it makes supply chains more efficient and effective. Now we need to build the regulatory highways that can take full advantage of the horsepower of modern supply chains and logistics in an ever-flattening world.

Are You Ready for the Flat World?

- How can managers understand and build their businesses around the mountains of a lumpy world?
- What national policies inhibit or promote network orchestration in your country or region?
- How can these policies be changed to facilitate more flexible supply chains?
- If the concept of "country of origin" is obsolete, how should we think about existing trade rules constructed along the lines of national borders?
- Given the need to reshape policy and practice in a world that is increasingly flat (but not completely flat), what do you need to do next?

12

Practice: A Lever to Move the World

Network orchestration and a broader view of the business can be applied in many different industries and organizations. At the same time, the world is not completely flat, so managers need to balance the thinking and models of the old round world with the opportunities and breakthrough approaches of the flat world.

Archimedes once said that if he had a lever long enough and a place to stand, he could move the whole world. Archimedes had no place to stand, so it remained a theoretical demonstration of a key principle of mechanics. But the flat world provides a platform. With independent streams of information and financial flows, the flat world gives us a place to stand and manage these flows separate from the physical world. Companies that can leverage this opportunity can truly move the world.

> **Archimedes once said if he had a lever long enough, he could move the world. He had no place to stand, but the flat world provides a platform.**

The emergence of linked global supply and logistics networks gives us a lever long enough to move the world. Customers who can tap into these new business models and strategies can harness the power of this networked world. Companies that can better orchestrate these global networks can build value for themselves and for their customers. These loosely linked networks are moving to a point at which they can deliver almost any product on demand from anywhere to anywhere in the world. A customer thinks about a new product and literally *moves the world* to deliver on this thought.

The orchestrator is the fulcrum, the center around which this lever moves, translating the desires of customers into actions in a far-flung global network of thousands of suppliers in every part of the globe. The implications of this shift extend far beyond manufacturing. Any company participating in networks—which is almost every company—needs to look at whether its current approaches are designed for this world. In this chapter, we examine some of the ways organizations in diverse industries are using networked models to move the world.

Rethinking the Business

In its 2007 survey of the top-performing companies in ten economic sectors, *Business Week* noted that these companies are taking a fresh look at their business models and industries. They are "rewriting the rules in their industries. They are the agitators, the pioneers, and the game-changers that are leading the way in the 21st century."[46] They include companies such as Google and Amazon, which have introduced networked business models for a wired world; brand builders such as Coach, which has built a customer-centric business in handbags, interviewing more than 60,000 of its customers each year; Nucor, which has used acquisitions, new technology, and employee relationships to propel its progress in the competitive steel industry; and the highly networked global business of Avon Products, which recruited nearly 400,000 salespeople in China in a single year. Many of these companies are orchestrating networks of customers, researchers, and suppliers to achieve rapid growth and high performance.

Not all companies can directly apply the network orchestration model that Li & Fung has used. But companies can think more broadly about their businesses and the chains that build the value they create. Li & Fung developed its principles of network orchestration in the context of global manufacturing, but these principles can help any enterprise take advantage of the opportunities of a flat world. The principles of competing network against network and taking a broader view of value creation can help expand the thinking and actions of almost any type of business.

The Flat World Requires Network Orchestration

The flat world allows for connecting and coordinating networks across the globe. No company can act alone in this world. No firm is an island, no matter how remote or far removed. No single individual or firm can master all the expertise needed to compete in a flat world, but they can connect to this expertise by creating broader networks. The walls are coming down.

> *The vertically integrated firm has disintegrated. To keep it from devolving into a cacophony of independent parts, an orchestrator must stand at the front.*

The vertically integrated firm has disintegrated. This is a tremendous opportunity. But this flattening and democratization of the world could lead to chaos and inefficiencies without some new form of coordination. The old management structures that General Motors invented years ago are no longer suited to this world. The high failure rates of strategic alliances, outsourcing, and offshoring indicate that an ingredient is missing in how we are approaching the management of these dispersed networks. The missing ingredient is network orchestration. Producing products and delivering services is not a solo performance in a flat world. It is a complex symphony, drawing together diverse instruments to deliver it. To keep it from devolving into a cacophony of independent parts, an orchestrator must stand at the front.

Opportunities for Network Orchestration

In a flat world, many opportunities arise to apply the insights of network orchestration to businesses beyond manufacturing. For example, Olam International has developed a model for agricultural products similar to Li & Fung's by focusing on the supply chain for agricultural and food products. Olam started in Nigeria in 1989, focusing on cashew nuts and later cotton, ginger, and sheanuts; incorporated in Singapore in 1995; and later shifted its base to London. With revenues of more than US$4 billion in 2006, it has become a leading global integrated supply chain manager for agricultural products and food ingredients. It has more than 5,000 employees in 40 countries. Olam purchases goods from small to medium-size farmers around the world, particularly in Asia and Africa. It accounts for 10 percent market share of the world's cotton production, 13 percent of cocoa, and about 25 percent of cashews. Olam also trades in coffee, rice, sugar, timber, spices, and beans. In addition to trading in agricultural products, Olam offers customers high-end services such as organic certification.[47]

> In a flat world, many opportunities arise to apply the insights of network orchestration to businesses beyond manufacturing.

Olam does not own farms, but instead concentrates on orchestrating a network of many small producers. This global network is geographically dispersed in both sourcing and sales. As an asset-light company, Olam's return on equity (ROE) was nearly 20 percent in 2005, with an even higher ROE in preceding years. This model has allowed it to grow quickly, posting a 21 percent compound annual growth rate (CAGR) in revenue from 2000 to 2005, and a 41 percent CAGR in net profit in the same period. Olam International has set stretch goals to double profits every three years over the next six years. It initially concentrated on organic growth, by expanding sourcing and markets or moving into adjacent products. But in 2006, it launched its first major inorganic growth initiative, joint ventures for cotton and soy beans in China with Chinatex, the leader in these commodities in China. If network orchestration can work for products as diverse as agricultural commodities, garments, and toys, this model can be applied to many different industries.

On a smaller scale, other networks for agriculture have brought together small farmers for specific purposes. For example, Thomas Friedman describes Kenyan company Advanced Bio-Extracts (ABE) that has brought together 7,000 small farmers in Kenya, Tanzania, and Uganda to grow artemisia (also called "sweet wormwood"), a key component in antimalaria drugs known as ACT therapies. The network allows the farmers to earn more than four times the yield of growing corn and connect with global investors and pharmaceutical companies, such as Swiss-based Novartis, while helping to fight one of the most deadly diseases on the African continent.[48]

Google's Bus Network: Taking a Broader View of the Business

Non-manufacturing companies also are building value by taking a broader view of the inputs to their own value chains. For example, one of the key inputs for Google's business is engineering and IT talent. Instead of just looking at this talent when it walks in the door every morning, Google began to realize that it could build and capture more value by looking at its employees before they arrive at the office and after they walk out the door at night.

This broader thinking led the company to establish a bus network in California with 230 miles of routes, more than twice as large as the public BART (Bay Area Rapid Transit) commuter train system, carrying more than 1,200 of its employees to and from its "Googleplex" headquarters in Mountain View. The service, created with a partner, not only is a valuable perk used to attract top talent, but also gives employees hours of extra productive time each day in vehicles with wireless Internet connections, time that would otherwise be wasted stuck in traffic on California's notorious freeways.[49] Just as manufacturers have looked past the doors of the factory to capture the "soft dollars," as discussed in Chapter 9, "Capturing the 'Soft $3' by Looking Beyond the Factory," Google is looking past the doors of its own company to build and capture more value in its own "supply chain."

This type of solution comes only from looking beyond the narrow confines of the business itself. How can you take a broader view of your own business? In what ways can you build value by looking beyond the business as it is currently defined? How can you orchestrate more of the network that creates value?

Building Collaborative Networks to Strike Gold

Many businesses offer the opportunity to tap into networks to access knowledge to create new products or find solutions to business challenges. Just as Li & Fung and other network orchestrators create networks to provide a pool of suppliers with manufacturing capabilities to flexibly provide customer solutions, other companies build and harness different networks to support their businesses. For example, in *Wikinomics: How Mass Collaboration Changes Everything*, Don Tapscott and Anthony Williams describe how Toronto-based gold-mining company Goldcorp, Inc., used an open innovation approach to drastically improve results.[50]

Like others in the industry, the company had fiercely protected its knowledge and relied upon internal geologists to direct its drilling. CEO Rob McEwen, inspired by the open-source software movement, decided to take a different approach. In March 2000, he offered a $575,000 prize to the person who could develop the best methods and estimates for where to look for gold on his 55,000-acre Canadian property. He posted all the company data about the site on the Internet. The contest drew more than 1,000 people from 50 countries, and they identified many new targets, 80 percent of which yielded substantial quantities of gold. The company estimated that the process shaved off two to three years from exploration, and Goldcorp grew from a $100 million company to a $9 billion firm.

Technology companies have been among the first and most aggressive adopters in harnessing the power of networks of developers and customers. For example, Slim Devices, which makes networked devices for streaming music throughout the home, draws together a global community of customers and developers who collaborate with staff in developing and refining its software and products. It offers its prerelease software for download every night and has set up a wiki to support collaboration of the community. Community members contribute their own software, which is also available for download.

Such "mass collaboration" draws upon the wisdom of a broader network. As noted in Chapter 8, "Follow the 30/70 Rule to Create Loose-Tight Organizations," Procter & Gamble has used research networks to identify and harness the creative ideas of more than a million entrepreneurs and inventors. It taps into these networks through a sophisticated system for orchestration. The company has a network of some 70 "technology entrepreneurs" around the world, senior P&G staff who identify technology needs and solutions, and build connections with academic and industry researchers in their regions. The company also taps into the research of its suppliers (its top 50 suppliers have a collective staff of 50,000 researchers) through an IT platform that allows P&G to share technology briefs with suppliers. Finally, it ties into open innovation networks such as Nine-Sigma and InnoCentive to look more broadly for ideas. P&G has actively built and managed a complex research network that has significantly improved its R&D performance and led to new blockbuster ideas. It is no longer competing firm and against firm, but is competing network against network. What are the opportunities to create and tap into broader networks for innovation in your own business? How can you identify or establish these networks? What skills are needed to manage them?

Orchestrating Consumer and Social Networks

Even as it was rethinking its R&D processes, Procter & Gamble took a networked approach to marketing. It called upon networks of "buzz agents" to serve as an auxiliary sales force. In 2001, it started Tremor, a project that drew together a quarter million teenagers to help pitch products of P&G (and other companies) to their friends. In 2005, it launched Vocalpoint, a word-of-mouth program that grew to more than 600,000 mothers who shared samples, coupons, and opinions with their friends.[51]

These networks are a way to organize and tap into the personal advocacy that has always been a powerful part of marketing. Companies such as Apple, with its MacWorld revival meetings and evangelists, have done this in a less structured way in the past. By creating more formal networks, P&G and others are starting to actively orchestrate word of mouth.

These examples also demonstrate how network orchestrators can tap into existing social networks in building their own networks. For example, the family networks of more than 50 million overseas Chinese have been a tremendous force in building businesses across Asia, including Li & Fung's (when it built a regional sourcing network in Southeast Asia in its first steps to globalize).[52] Technology networks often include gurus around which others have organized. In choosing participants in its Vocalpoint network, P&G looked for members with many relationships with other mothers—nodes of their own networks. Network orchestrators can recognize and connect to these natural networks to increase the power and reach of their own networks.

Nike + iPod: Innovative Combinations

Just as global networks have created opportunities to combine capabilities from different regions (such as plush dolls and sophisticated speech chips to create talking dolls), a networked world offers new possibilities to combine very different capabilities to produce innovative products. For example, iPod and Nike combined forces for the Nike + iPod training system. Recognizing that many runners and other athletes already are taking their iPods along, Apple and Nike have created a whole system that serves as a personal trainer.

The system starts with a pair of specially designed Nike sneakers with a built-in pocket under the insole to hold a sensor that communicates with the iPod. Nike also makes special apparel with pockets to hold the iPod and the receiver for the sensor. The next part of the system is the iPod Nano, which not only provides a soundtrack for the workout, but also tracks workout data. Finally, a Nike + iPod Sports Kit (which includes a sensitive accelerometer that measures activity and wirelessly transmits data to the iPod) draws the whole system together. This system allows athletes to track their time and miles, hear feedback on their training, and listen to their favorite music. The music can even be organized and synchronized to the workout. After running, the athlete can sync up information with a computer through the iPod to track runs, analyze performance, set goals, and challenge friends anywhere in the world at www.nikeplus.com.

This is the kind of collaboration that is not possible without a networked view. It allows Nike to tap into the networks of iPod customers and iPod to tap into Nike's customer network. It draws together expertise in running shoes and apparel with expertise in consumer electronics, while capitalizing on two powerful brands. Bringing together these two capabilities and groups of customers creates something that neither company could have created independently.

Network orchestration is having an impact in many other areas. In sports leagues, such as the U.K. Premier League in football (soccer), clubs and players gain value from being part of the league. Managers and players are sourced from all over the world, and merchandising and TV rights are handled via a global network. This has led to considerable wealth creation. This regional network is then part of a global sports network such as FIFA that draws together teams in various countries for events such as the World Cup. These are networks within networks, and these connections help to build value for all those involved.

Beyond Business

Although our focus has been primarily on how businesses need to compete in this world, the flat world obviously has many implications for organizations beyond businesses. It is having a dramatic impact on reengineering and reinventing government, military organizations, society, and its institutions.

Even the military has turned to its own networks for counterterrorism and defense in this complex world of decentralized global terrorist networks. These

> *The flat world obviously has many implications for organizations beyond businesses.*

networks include the emergence of new players such as Blackwater, a U.S.-based private firm that provides experienced military personnel, support, and training to countries and organizations around the globe. This company can assemble forces quickly to provide protection for heads of state and support international organizations or even nations by assembling "trained personnel" from around the world. These companies collaborate with other companies, such as Antov in the Ukraine, to provide vital heavy airlifting capability for logistical support. In a world of decentralized and unpredictable threats, due to well orchestrated terrorist networks, counterterrorist intelligence and response also need to be quicker and more adaptable. This requires better network orchestration. Military and antiterrorist forces are, in fact, competing "network against network" against Al Qaeda and other terrorist organizations. The conventional command-and-control approaches, with wholly owned resources that once defined national military forces, are increasingly giving way to network orchestration.

Network orchestration also has implications for NGOs (non-governmental organizations) and other nonprofits. These organizations have always drawn upon broad networks for support, but they are currently much more active in collaborating with government and business to achieve their objectives. Public-private models, such as those used in microlending, demonstrate the power of such networks in creating markets to direct aid where it is needed most, while creating sustainable enterprises.

Nobel Prize winner Muhammad Yunus pioneered microfinancing through his Grameen Bank, but now new and flatter models are emerging. Sites, such as www.kiva.org, enable individuals who want to invest in entrepreneurial businesses in the developing world to make small loans to people they have never met. The photos, loan proposals, and credit histories of potential recipients are posted online, and investors can make their loans to small bakeries or retailers online.[53] Using flat-world technology and connections, such models of orchestration can have a powerful impact in building developing economies by connecting global needs with global resources at the individual level. At the other extreme, we are seeing the emergence of networks of networks in microfinance. For example, Women's World Banking has created a network of 53 microfinance institutions in 30 countries throughout Asia, Africa, Eastern Europe, Latin America, and the Middle East that are providing microfinancing to women entrepreneurs.[54]

NGOs and private foundations are playing an increasingly important role in collaborating with governments and business. For example, the $100 computer project, spearheaded by MIT Media Lab founder Nicolas Negroponte, could play a significant role in advancing education in many developing markets. Foundations are also addressing a wide range of problems, from targeting AIDS and other health care crises to providing sanitation and clean water, that will play a role in supporting economic progress of emerging markets.

Striking a Balance in a Flat-Round World

In applying the principles of network orchestration presented in this book, managers need to recognize that they are not absolute. These principles for competing in the flat world need to be balanced against the demands of organizations in transition and a world that is not completely flat.

Every moment, managers need to weigh many demands and opportunities to make choices about their strategies. These decisions often have to be made in an environment of great complexity and uncertainty. Changing organizations takes time, and transforming broader business ecosystems can take even longer. The flat world is very much a work in progress. Because we live in a world in transition, for each of the principles of network orchestration discussed, managers need to balance the old way of thinking and old approaches with the new, as summerized in Table 12-1.

> *In a flat-round world, our actions need to balance the ideal and the reality, to take advantage of the opportunities the flat world presents without overlooking the limitations and opportunities of the round world. Managers need to strike a balance between opposing forces.*

TABLE 12-1   The World in the Balance

Principle	Required Balance Between	
	Round World and	Flat World
Orchestrate the network	Operation	Orchestration
Compete network against network	Focus on cost	Focus on performance
Take responsibility for the whole chain	Loose coupling	Tight controls
Empower "Little John Waynes"	Benefiting from the large organization	Acting entrepreneurially
Establish the three-year stretch	Stability	Renewal
Build the company around the customer	Meeting customer needs	Building a profitable business
Follow the 30/70 rule	Commitment	Flexibility
Capture the soft $3	Today's efficiency	Tomorrow's broader opportunities
Sell to the source	Sourcing	Marketing
Policy	Protecting national industries	Serving global consumers

Balancing Firm and Network

Companies are incorporated and organized as independent entities. Laws and regulations are built around this idea, as are standard principles of management. Yet in a networked world, the firm is not the right unit of analysis. We have to look to the network to understand how value is created. Managers need to be able to balance operational efficiency of the firm with orchestration of the network, balance a view of the independent company with a view of the broader network, and balance the flexibility of a loosely coupled network with the demand for control and compliance in a world that is increasingly concerned with corporate social responsibility. Among the balances that must be struck are:

- **Orchestrate the network—balancing operation and orchestration**: Command and control are eroding. Leaders in flat organizations are architects and orchestrators. They develop and refine the design of the organization. They work across disciplinary silos. At the same time, the success of the business at the end of the day depends on operational excellence—delivering the right product to the right place at the right time at the right price. Managers need to balance the flexibility of orchestration against the effectiveness and efficiency of operations.

- **Compete network against network—balancing your part against the whole**: In the old world, it was every firm for itself, but today it is one network against another. Instead of focusing on squeezing the most value from suppliers or buyers, or competing with a rival at one point in the chain, the focus should be on creating a better network than that of competitors. But managers cannot be completely altruistic in this process. They need to be sure that they can capture at least some of the benefits of this improved supply chain for their own company. They have to balance the demands of their own business and shareholders against contributing to optimizing the entire value chain.

Balancing Control and Empowerment

The corporation depends upon direct control over the enterprise, but as more of the work of the business, and the value created, migrates out to the network, empowerment becomes more important. Empowerment allows for more entrepreneurship, longer planning cycles, and stretch goals, organizing around the customer and building flexible, loose-tight networks of partners. These strategies of empowerment need to be balanced with traditional control systems:

- **Take responsibility for the whole chain—balancing loose coupling with tight controls**: Although networks are loosely coupled, they still need to adhere to tight standards and customer demands that are higher than ever. Networks do not depend upon top-down control. Instead, they thrive based on education, a clear set of rules, monitoring and standards. Communities need to develop a balance between control and independence, as can be seen in eBay's buyer and seller rating systems. Instead of the company serving as a policeman, members of the community rate past transactions with individuals, using the community itself to reinforce values and ensure the quality and integrity of transactions. The company created a framework for this to happen but does not try to micromanage the process. Managers need to strike a balance between rigid controls that could stifle creativity and initiative, and looseness that could lead to serious compromises in compliance and scandals that could affect all the members of the network.

- **Empower "Little John Waynes"—balancing acting entrepreneurially with benefiting from the large organization**: Entrepreneurship is crucial to success, so large organizations need to create an entrepreneurial culture while continuing to take advantage of the size of the parent organization. These "Little John Waynes" need to be able to circle the wagons and fight off the enemy on the ground, but still have access to the resources of the larger organization. Managers need to strike a balance between providing these entrepreneurial leaders with enough autonomy so they can serve customers effectively and creatively, and yet ensure that they are aligned with the culture of the parent company and benefit from its infrastructure and support.

- **Create the three-year stretch—balancing stability and renewal**: In a world of rapid change, organizations need to balance stability and renewal. The pressures of annual budgets and quarterly reporting lead to a short-term focus and reactive strategies. Five-year rolling plans very often lead to changes in objectives before managers can get initiatives rolling. Instead, Li & Fung sets bold objectives every three years and allows its entrepreneurial leaders to execute against these "goal posts" over a three-year period. Not every company will find the three-year plan to be the best fit for their businesses, but organizations need to find effective approaches to planning that balance stability and renewal. Stability gives individuals enough room to work but also ensures that the plan is periodically readjusted for a changing world.

- **Build the company around the customer—balancing customer needs with a profitable business**: To build your business, give it to your customers. The more the business focuses on the concerns of the customer and the customer's customer, the faster it will grow. Because the business itself is flexible, the design of a value chain or the business itself starts with the customer. In a certain sense, the company becomes second to the customer but still retains its separate identity. At the same time, the company needs to be conscious of building its own business. Which customers should it do business with to drive its own growth? How can it serve these customers profitably? Managers need to balance building their own business with centering on customers needs, engaging customers as partners in codevelopment of products, and cosourcing.

- **Follow the 30/70 rule—balancing commitment and flexibility**: Networks need to be both loose and tight. Members need enough independence so the network is flexible and always learning, but the commitment to the network needs to be sufficient so that players have a stake in its success. For Li & Fung, targeting between 30 and 70 percent of the capacity of its suppliers ensures commitment without absolute lock-in. But this represents a wide range of levels of commitment, so finding and sustaining the best level of commitment to a given supplier and supply chain requires careful balance and understanding of that supply, as well as the type of product being produced. Since the world is not completely flat, there may be industries and instances where more fixed relationships work better.

Balancing Specialization and Integration

Since Adam Smith's famous pin factory, specialization has allowed factories to increase their performance. Each task is done by a skilled expert, and the factory brings these specialists together to create value. But in a networked world, value is also created by integrating these specialized skills across a broader network. This allows companies to think beyond their own specialized part of the chain to

capture the "soft dollars" and to draw together marketing and operations insights to "sell to the source." Even so, managers need to balance these activities with more traditional approaches:

- **Capture the soft dollars—balancing efficiency today with
  pursuing broader opportunities**: Whatever your small part
  of the network is, take a broader view. The biggest opportunities
  in manufacturing are not in making improvements to the manufacturing plant, which might account for a few cents' improvement in the $1 manufacturing cost of a $4 toy. Instead, the
  biggest opportunities for creating value are in the rest of the
  value—the "soft $3" after the product leaves the plant. Improv-
  ing efficiencies in the factory is important, but this needs to be
  balanced with the opportunities from taking a more holistic
  view of value-creation opportunities outside the factory door.

- **Sell to the source—balancing sourcing and marketing**:
  Markets that sell also buy. Networks for sourcing can become
  networks for selling by leveraging expertise and knowledge of
  the source market. In organizations with many more edges, the
  opportunities might be much more multifaceted, but to capitalize on these opportunities, managers need to draw diverse
  insights together. In particular, the specialized insights of marketing and operations which are still vital to corporate success,
  need to be brought together to capitalize on their synergies.

Finally, these specific principles of network orchestration are all
interdependent, so managers need to balance all of them. The mindset of competing network against network affects the way managers
approach the organization of their business and relationships with
customers and suppliers. The shape of policy obviously influences the
capability of companies to build networks and global supply chains or
to engage in network orchestration. Overall, in a world that is more
loosely coupled, managers need greater skill in managing without the
rigid systems for control that vertically integrated and geographically
concentrated organizations have used. The principles of network
orchestration might appear quite simple, but the trade-offs implied
by the set of balances mean that implementation for any given business requires careful management decision making.

Participating in Networks

Not every player is a network orchestrator. Many firms are part of networks without orchestrating them. These companies need to develop skills in serving as members of networks. What kind of skills does its take to be a part of a network? Network members typically need to have some clearly defined product or capability that they bring to the table. They also need skills in managing relationships with the network orchestrator (or several orchestrators of different networks) and other partners. To protect their own profits, they need to be able to evaluate the benefits of being part of the network and recognize when those benefits could be reduced. Network participants need to pay particular attention to the idiosyncratic investments and other risks of participating in the network, and recognize when these risks increase or place their own businesses at significant risk.

Although they might not be orchestrating the network, these partners also need to be able to see the network through the eyes of the network orchestrator. How can value be created across the

> *Not every player is a network orchestrator. Many firms are part of networks without orchestrating them.*

network by competing network against network? How can the supplier or other partner increase the value it contributes to the network by thinking more broadly? How can it work with the network orchestrator to improve the overall efficiency and effectiveness of the network, and then share the value that is created? Are there opportunities for the network partner to expand its role in network orchestration? For example, a player in the network might create subassemblies or take on more responsibility for orchestrating the part of the chain around its own business.

A successful orchestra requires more than a great conductor. It requires the active participation of every musician in every seat. Playing in an orchestra or participating in a network requires a distinctive set of skills in addition to ability with a particular musical instrument or stage of the production process. The network is more than just a collection of separate players, so its overall performance depends upon the networking skills of all the players.

Leading Networks

Networks also require a distinctive approach to leadership. We have discussed the entrepreneurial leadership needed by the "Little John Waynes" who head up specific customer-facing businesses, but network orchestrators also have to consider the leadership needed across the firm. Leaders need to be able to empower strong and independent-minded entrepreneurs. Leaders need to build the confidence of all members of the network to help them understand that they benefit if the network benefits. This requires a certain level of humility and flexibility in leaders, as well as strong listening skills.

To remain flexible and work globally, leaders also have to be willing to absorb and adapt to the diverse cultures of the network. Hong Kong has always been an international city, so Li & Fung has had many years to understand and adapt to a multicultural environment.

> *Network orchestration requires a certain level of humility and flexibility in leaders, as well as an openness to diversity, attentiveness to changes in the environment, and integrity.*

Leaders need to be able to speak with a retailer in New York one minute and a supplier in Indonesia the next. Leaders need to develop not only a tolerance for diversity, but an appreciation for it. Leaders need to address corporate cultures and practices, industry culture, national culture, and the culture of the regional or international organizations to which the country belongs (EU or NAFTA, for example).

Li & Fung has combined the values and culture of a traditional Chinese company with modern Western theories and principles of management, and learned from the cultures and practices of the companies it has collaborated with and acquired. In working in diverse parts of the world, local solutions are often distinctly tailored to the needs of a specific region. And with an open mind, the network orchestrator can learn something from everyone who participates in the network. By listening to and gathering the best wisdom and best practices of the network, leaders continue to improve their own organizations and the entire network.

Leaders need to be carefully attuned to the changing world. They need to be aware of rising concerns such as human rights or environmental issues, and to think about their implications for their own enterprises and networks. They must be willing to change their own mental models continuously and encourage the organization to take a fresh look at the business. How much should the network orchestrator push suppliers to be early adopters of new environmental practices? These changes could entail significant costs, but it might be better to implement them before they are imposed from the outside. To keep an ear to the ground, leaders need to look beyond their own businesses to play an active role in their community and the world, from meeting with political and economic leaders to participating in organizations such as The Nature Conservancy. Leaders of networks often are in the best position to see where the world is headed and to mobilize the entire network to meet emerging challenges.

Finally, leaders of networked enterprises need to have integrity and trust. This is the foundation of network orchestration. They need to develop trust with customers, with suppliers, and within the organization. This integrity and trust will hold together loosely linked organizations and networks, align these networks around common goals, slice through complexity, and smooth the bumps along the way.

An Ever-Flattening World

The world is growing flatter every day. New developments continue to push the limits of technology and redefine what we mean by a network. The emergence of online communities such as MySpace and YouTube, or the growth of simulated environments such as Second Life, have created new platforms for a very different way of interacting and sharing information. What implications do these developments have for global business? What will future networks look like? Just as it was difficult to anticipate how the Internet and other innovations would affect the last generation of networks, we need to think carefully about how these innovations will affect our future networks.

The changes in technology and the flattening of the world all present new challenges and opportunities. We need to recognize how the world is getting flatter and how its shape is being transformed.

We need to change our mental models to understand this world and see the opportunities it presents. We need to think about the implications of these changes for our businesses. How can we use the new approaches? How can we build adaptive experiments to test new business models or approaches that might work in this new world? How can we challenge our current mental models to allow us to see the opportunities in these changes?

We have learned many lessons from competing in a flat world. But these are the lessons of the past. Li & Fung is a very different organization than it was a couple decades ago. What will the future of Li & Fung look like? What will the future of your business look like? We need to continue to pay attention to the lessons that the flat world teaches us and act quickly to understand and act upon their implications.

Are You Ready for the Flat World?

- Given the specific demands and constraints of your industry, what are the opportunities for network orchestration?
- How are you achieving a balance in your own business in each of the principles of network orchestration discussed in this chapter?
- Are you a network orchestrator or part of a network? Do you have an opportunity to become a network orchestrator?
- What kind of leadership do you need in a flat world with increasing orchestration?
- Given the demands of the flat world, what do you need to do next?

Conclusion _____

Are You Ready to Compete Flat Out?

In March 2007, the news broke that ITT Corp. had agreed to pay a fine to the U.S. government of up to $100 million for exporting classified technology for night-vision goggle component parts to China, Singapore, and Britain in 2001. The sensitive night-vision technology was critical to the success of U.S. forces in Iraq and other battlefields, allowing U.S. troops to "own the night." The breach was considered one that could put soldiers on the battlefield at risk.

Outsourcing was at the heart of the case. ITT's Night Vision unit arranged to have various components of its goggles made by contract manufacturers in Asia. Managers were looking for a lower-cost manufacturer of the goggle's light interference filter after its California manufacturer refused to lower its price. The search for a new manufacturer delayed a key order, so an ITT manager sent drawings and technical data to a company in Singapore, who outsourced fabrication to its facilities in the People's Republic of China.[55] Although this is common practice for companies such as Dell, it requires a government license for military hardware. ITT had not obtained this license.

The company stressed that the violation under the International Traffic in Arms Regulation (ITFAR) had not revealed its core technology of the goggles, although it admitted to transferring the technology without receiving advance approval. ITT put into place new internal controls, including ethics classes for employees, a new compliance officer, and better tracking systems.

The case points out the particularly sticky challenges facing companies in specific industries as they seek to apply the principles of network orchestration. Although few industries are as tightly regulated as military hardware, a balance always exists between creating networks and building transparency versus protecting the integrity of the knowledge of the firm—or, in this case, a nation. As the world becomes flatter, networks become more important. As networks become more important, so does network orchestration. But every company and every industry needs to determine how to apply these principles, given its specific opportunities and constraints. How can you apply these principles to your business?

> *As networks become more important, so does network orchestration. But every company and every industry needs to determine how to apply these principles.*

A Plan for Action

In discussing the concepts of the book with business executives, they identified their most pressing challenges: If you accept the premise that today's managers have to address Thomas Friedman's evolving flat world and the older reality that much of the world is not flat, what should you do next? How do you ensure that you will achieve your objectives, especially profitable growth? Do you have the competencies to achieve these objectives? We examine each of these questions, forming a foundation for a plan of action to respond to the challenge of the flat world.

What Should You Do Next?

What do you need to do next to respond to the demands of the flat world? The first order of business is to challenge your current mental models.[56] Mental models shape what we are able to see and how we are able to act. To recognize new threats or see new opportunities, we need to challenge and often change our mental models. Given the changes of the evolving flat world, do your mental models still work? If you are still looking at the world through the lens of the firm, how do you need to shift your thinking to understand the opportunities of the network?

When you recognize that the world is changing, to what extent are the forces Thomas Friedman describes affecting your own business environment? Given that we live in a world that is becoming *flatter* but is still a mix of flat and unflat, how is your own business environment being reshaped? The constraints of specific industries and businesses, as illustrated by the ITT night vision case, also affect how these forces play out. What type of businesses and strategies are likely to succeed in this new complex world?

Examine the gaps in the readiness of your own organization to compete in this world. Where is your organization today on the spectrum between the traditional firm and network orchestrator (as discussed in Chapter 1, "The Orchestration Imperative")? Identify your firm's position on each of the three dimensions shown in Figure C-1. What is the balance between the focus on the firm and the focus on the network? What is the balance between management by control and management by empowerment? What is the balance between value creation based on specialization and value creation based on integration? Then, for each dimension, consider where your firm *should be* to compete effectively in this flat world. How can you close these gaps?

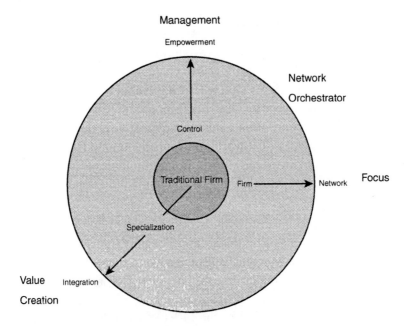

FIGURE C-1 Network orchestration

How Do You Achieve Profitable Growth?

The flat world offers tremendous opportunities for growth. Companies have developed new business models to meet more empowered consumers. They are utilizing new technologies to rethink production to cut costs and improve quality. The flat world opens up new markets, particularly in emerging economies. But the flat world also introduces fierce new competitors that can appear from the remotest corners of the globe, making it more challenging to achieve *profitable* growth. This world presents significant opportunities and risks.

Emerging markets account for 86 percent of the world's population and represent the fastest-growing markets on the planet, as Vijay Mahajan and Kamini Banga note in their book *The 86% Solution*.[57] But these markets require different insights and market strategies than the 14 percent of the global population in the developed world. As C. K. Prahalad demonstrates, with the right models, opportunities exist even among the poorest segments of these markets, "at the bottom of the pyramid."[58]

In addition to emerging markets, managers need to look at the opportunities created by more empowered consumers. These consumers drive their purchase by search. They expect speed, customization and an increasingly active role in interactions with companies. Companies that can build supply chains and networks to respond to these new demands can capitalize on the opportunities presented by these consumers. [59] Companies need the expertise to create new solutions, but they are often limited by their own capabilities. Network orchestration gives organizations access to the capabilities they need to compete. This allows companies to deliver the right product to the right place at the right time at the right price—from virtually anywhere in the world to virtually anywhere in the world. It connects the emerging opportunities of global markets with the global capabilities needed to serve them.

> *Network orchestration connects the emerging opportunities of global markets with the global capabilities needed to serve them.*

Network orchestration can help to seize the opportunities for growth and manage the risks. It is scalable, which facilitates growth. At the same time, it is flexible, so the network can respond to changing conditions.

How Can You Build the Competencies You Need to Compete?

What competencies do you need to successfully compete in this world today and sustain your competitiveness in the future? In their breakthrough work on core competencies, C. K. Prahalad and Gary Hamel identified a firm's core competencies as a critical source of competitive advantage.[60] A core competency is something a company can do well (a capability) that is difficult for competitors to imitate and that can be leveraged across many products and markets. Companies can build on and extend these core competencies to grow their business, as Honda used its expertise in small engines to move from motorcycles to automobiles, to lawnmowers, to snowblowers. The idea is to use core competencies not just to protect one vertical, but to leverage these core competencies in a number of verticals. In making outsourcing decisions, conventional wisdom is that companies should closely hold their core competencies and access less critical capabilities from best-in-class providers. Based on this firm-centric view of competencies, your company is as strong as the core competencies it possesses.

But as we move toward a network-centric world, we need to take a fresh look at core competencies. The company's strength lies not as much in the competencies that it *possesses* as much as in the competencies it can *connect to*. This means that the capability to connect to competencies—the capability for network orchestration—and the capability for learning might be becoming as important as any firm-specific capabilities in capitalizing on the opportunities of a flat, networked world. Whereas capabilities in sewing and production would appear to be crucial to a successful garment business, the Li & Fung model has shown that a company does not have to hold these capabilities in-house. In fact, the company has more flexibility by connecting with these capabilities instead of holding them centrally. Network orchestration, like other core competencies, can be applied across diverse markets and industries. Li & Fung has applied this core competency to a variety of products, such as garments, toys, and auto parts.

> *The company's strength lies not as much in the competencies that it possesses as much as in the competencies it can connect to. This means that the capability to connect to competencies—the capability for network orchestration—and the capability for learning might be becoming as important as any firm-specific capabilities.*

How can you build a competency in network orchestration? This book provides a blueprint. Review each of the principles presented in the book and answer the following questions to identify your strengths and weaknesses in each area.

Firm and Network

The first challenge in building a capacity for network orchestration is shifting perspective from the firm to the network. The network orchestrator does not compete firm against firm, but views competition as network against network.

Orchestrate the Network (Chapter 2)

- Does your company serve as the hub and organizer of a value network?

- Are you engaged in network orchestration in addition to supply chain management?

- Do you have a rich global network that can respond quickly and effectively to every customer demand?

Compete Network Against Network (Chapter 3)

- Do you focus on optimizing the entire network and building relationships with supply chain partners rather than competing firm against firm and creating adversarial relationships with supply and process chain partners?

- Do you clearly identify the networks that support your competitors and understand how your own network compares to theirs?

- Do you offshore or outsource not only for cost savings, but to connect with the best capabilities in the best locations in the world?

Control and Empowerment

The next challenge in creating a capability for network orchestration is to balance the need for control of the overall system and the need to empower loosely coupled networks and entrepreneurial leaders.

Take Responsibility for the Whole Chain (Chapter 4)

- Do you have structures and processes in place to allow you to monitor compliance with human rights, environmental, and other regulations through the dispersed network?

- Have you developed the education and support to allow suppliers to be successful in meeting standards?

- Do you have the information and controls to know whether every part of your dispersed network meets standards for compliance in real time?

Empower "Little John Waynes" (Chapter 5)

- Are your organization, culture, incentives, and other drivers designed to encourage leaders of business units to act autonomously and entrepreneurially?
- Do you have plug-and-play resources to support these entrepreneurs to free them up to focus on their customers and business?
- Are you effective in identifying, developing, and retaining entrepreneurial managers in your organization?

Establish a Three-Year Stretch (Chapter 6)

- Does your planning processes use zero-based, fixed plans versus rolling plans?
- Do you create stretch goals that drive creative thinking and growth?
- Do you reward managers for growth but not penalize them for falling short of stretch goals (to encourage them to set true stretches)?

Build the Company Around the Customer (Chapter 7)

- Is your organization structured around customers rather than your internal business units or functions?
- Do customers feel your organization is part of their own organization?
- Have you created thick connections with customers based on both technology and personal relationships?

Follow the 30/70 Rule (Chapter 8)

- Do you have a significant part of the business of each of your suppliers, but not their whole business?
- Do you allow your suppliers flexibility and learn from their interactions with other customers?
- Do you share information with suppliers and gain insights from them?

Specialization and Integration

Value creation in the traditional firm is based on specialization of firms and within the firm. For the network orchestrator, value creation is based on integration within the firm and across firms. This integration means looking across the chain to find opportunities to capture the "soft dollars" after manufacturing, and bringing together marketing and operations within the firm to capture opportunities to "sell to the source."

Capture the Soft Dollars (Chapter 9)

- Do you understand the stages of the supply chain, the value that is created, and the costs incurred at each stage?
- Do you look for profit opportunities in parts of the value chain where your firm is not currently playing?
- Do you expand your view of the business to capture these opportunities across the chain?

Sell to the Source (Chapter 10)

- Are there opportunities to sell to the same emerging markets where you source from?
- Are your selling and sourcing in emerging markets tightly coordinated to provide insights on the emergence of retail markets and synergies between manufacturing and marketing?
- Do you bridge the silos between your marketing and operations functions, and other parts of the organization?

A New World View

The flat world challenges our view of the firm, our view of management, and our models for value creation. In short, it challenges our entire view of what a business is and how it should be run. Just as the idea of the round world allowed Christopher Columbus to set sail across the Atlantic Ocean, the breakthrough idea of the flat world Thomas Friedman proposes opens new possibilities for businesses that are prepared to rise to this challenge.

> *The flat world challenges our entire view of what a business is and how it should be run.*

The specific principles of network orchestration discussed previously do not stand alone. They should be seen as part of this broader shift in thinking from a round world to a flat world, from the firm to network orchestration. All of these components are aspects of that broader picture.

Finally, it is one thing to understand this bigger picture, but success at network orchestration, as in all business, depends on consistent execution. This is all the more challenging, given the increased complexity—the many moving parts—of networked enterprises. Whereas a successful company in the past might have been like a lone sprinter or marathon runner, the successful network orchestrator is in a complex relay race where speed and surefootedness are important, but so is the gracefulness of passing the baton.

Most of our laws and trade policies are designed for the round world, in which national regulations and bilateral agreements shaped the playing field, as discussed in Chapter 11, "Policy: Building a Borderless Business in a World of Nation-States." If countries stand still, they could be left behind. But they also do not want to give up national advantages and they want to protect their own jobs and wealth. How can they protect military secrets while benefiting from global manufacturing? How do regulations and thoughts about global trade need to change? As with companies, the future will not be defined by every country for itself against the world; instead, future success will depend upon building and orchestrating networks.

Beyond the challenges to the design and management of companies, the flat world raises broader challenges about societal wealth
creation and distribution. Will this improve with the rise of networks,
or will the disparities become more pronounced? The transparency
of networks has the potential to create friction among different players in different parts of the world. How will these tensions be managed? The results depend not only on the development of network
orchestration and new business models, but also on the decisions of
policymakers in wrestling with the implications of the flat world.

An Evolving World

By its nature, the networked firm is fluid and evolving. It will not
stand still. Each new node that is added to the network has the potential to change the network itself. Small players in remote parts of the
world, in your own network, or outside your network, could force you
to rethink your business model. Certainly, Li & Fung's own business
will continue to change as the flat-world terrain continues to present
new opportunities and as new technology and business models for
seizing these opportunities are developed.

In the 100 years since its founding, Li & Fung has been transformed many times. In fact, it is an organization that is now designed
for transformation. Some of the lessons about culture, trust, and relationships that go back to the start of the Li & Fung business have not
changed in the century since its founding. Other aspects of the firm,
such as the business model that has shifted from agent to orchestrator, have changed in fundamental ways. These transformations will
continue and probably accelerate in the years ahead.

The principles of network orchestration described here will form
the foundation for the next evolution of the firm, its management, and
value creation, just as the flat world of Globalization 3.0 will form the
basis for Globalization 4.0. The first sketchy lines of these new organizations are already being drawn today. The principles of network
orchestration that we have developed and implemented at Li & Fung
will continue to evolve as the world changes. From all the signs, it is

From all the signs, it is clear that networks will play an increasingly important role in the future of our global enterprises. And that means network orchestration will be more important than ever to survival and success.

clear that networks will play an increasingly important role in the future of our global enterprises. And that means network orchestration will be more important than ever to survival and success.

To share your insights on competing in the flat world or your thoughts on the book, please visit the authors' web site at www.competinginaflatworld.net.

Appendix _____

About Li & Fung

Founded in Guangzhou, PRC, in 1906, the Li & Fung Group is a multinational group of companies driving strong growth in three distinct core businesses: export sourcing through Li & Fung Limited, distribution through integrated distribution services (IDS), and retailing through Convenience Retail Asia (CRA) and other nonlisted entities. The Li & Fung Group has a total staff of more than 24,000 across 40 countries worldwide, with revenues of more than US$8.7 billion in 2006.

The Group's export trading arm, the primary focus of this book, is Li & Fung Limited, one of the world's largest export sourcing firms. It manages the supply chain of high-volume, time-sensitive consumer goods through its office network in close to 40 countries. The Group's retailing business, including the publicly traded CRA Ltd., Toys "R" Us, and Branded Lifestyle and Licensing, has store networks extending from the Greater China markets to Singapore, Malaysia, Thailand, Indonesia, and South Korea. The Group's distribution business is housed under the IDS Group, which provides its customers a menu of integrated distribution services in three core businesses across Asia: manufacturing, logistics, and marketing.

In 1906, Fung Pak-liu (grandfather of Victor and William Fung) founded Li & Fung in Canton (now Guangzhou). It was one of the first companies set up by Chinese merchants to engage directly in foreign trade with foreign countries. Li & Fung's principal line of business in those days was exporting handicraft products made in China to the West. At that time, no one could have predicted the historical events that would transform the Chinese mainland and Hong Kong several times over the next 100 years. The first big change came with the Sino-Japanese war in the 1930s, when Fung Pak-liu moved company headquarters to Hong Kong. It was not easy to set down new roots, but Hong Kong, with its deep sea port, was the port of entry to southern China. In establishing Li & Fung so early in what was to become one of the great trading cities of the world, he built a solid legacy of experience and values for succeeding generations.

In 1949, just as Fung Pak-liu passed the reins of management to the second generation, Li & Fung's business environment suffered a devastating external shock. For 30 years, from 1949 to 1979, the Chinese mainland was basically isolated from the world, implying that Hong Kong had lost its hinterland and Li & Fung had lost its production base. The second generation of Li & Fung management—Fung Hon-chu (father of Victor and William Fung); his brother, Fung Moying; and his sister, Fung Laiwah—had to once again reinvent the company. Luckily, the wave of industrialists arriving in Hong Kong from Shanghai and other places in China after the change of government in 1949 established the British colony as a base for light manufacturing for export. In fact, this was the beginning of the globalization of labor-intensive manufacturing. Instead of trading in Chinese handicraft products, Li & Fung set to work with these new business partners to export consumer goods, such as garments, toys, and household products, made in Hong Kong, to Western markets. The business model that Fung Hon-chu and his siblings tirelessly implemented succeeded and brought great prosperity to Li & Fung from 1949 to 1972.

In the early 1970s, when Victor and William Fung returned from studies abroad and entered management as the third generation, Hong Kong and Li & Fung were facing a crisis. Competing Asian tiger economies were rising fast as lower-cost production locations, and major Western retailers were engaging increasingly in direct trade with their Asian suppliers. In this new environment, the model of exporting goods made in Hong Kong had run its course. In the business school sense, it was time for Li & Fung to reinvent itself. Victor and William Fung decided to seek out new opportunities and to offer new kinds of value-added services to major U.S. retailers, identifying the best production bases in Asia and assisting with their overall Asian sourcing activities. First, Li & Fung went regional, opening operations in Taiwan, Korea, and many other countries in Southeast Asia, taking care to organize the company's operations around the needs of its customers. In the late 1970s, with the advent of the economic reform, the opening of the Chinese mainland by Deng Xiaoping, and the creation of special economic zones, a big part of its factory base moved to the mainland of China.

Li & Fung was heavily involved in developing the concept of global supply chain management in its early days. Over the next several decades, the company developed capabilities upstream, midstream, and downstream across the supply chain. It separated the sourcing of raw material and components from finding the right locations for the labor-intensive assembly, and it developed practical solutions for quick-response manufacturing, making products shop-ready at the factory level. All in all, it created a comprehensive strategy for global supply chain management. From 1992 to 2006, the turnover of Li & Fung Limited, the Group's export company and core business, grew at a compound annual growth rate of more than 22 percent. Today the Li & Fung Group (including Li & Fung Limited, IDS, Circle K convenience stores under CRA, and other private entities) has embarked on a whole new era of globalization. This globalization will take Li & Fung into a world where the supply chain extends outward toward the developed markets of the world and also connects back into the markets of China and Southeast Asia. Li & Fung has a very open architecture and culture that enables it to work with people from different parts of the world.

Notes

1. Thomas Friedman, *The World Is Flat: A Brief History of the 21st Century* (London: Allen Lane, 2005).

2. John Hagel and John Seely Brown introduced the term "process orchestrator" in their articles and book *The Only Sustainable Edge: Why Business Strategy Depends on Productive Friction and Dynamic Specialization* (Boston: Harvard Business School Press, 2005), based on Li & Fung's model. Earlier, Peter Drucker used the conductor and the orchestra to describe leadership with the flattening of the organization.

3. Although the staff of the entire Li & Fung Group (including trading, retailing, and distribution) is 24,000, staff of Li & Fung Trading Group (or Li & Fung Limited) is about 10,000, with 2006 revenues for the group just over US$8.7 billion. References to Li & Fung throughout the book refer to Li & Fung trading operations.

4. Among many articles are an interview with Victor Fung in *Harvard Business Review* ("Fast, Global and Entrepreneurial: Supply Chain Management, Hong Kong Style," by Joan Magretta, September-October 1998), and a series of Harvard Business School case studies between 1996 and the present (including 9-396-075, N1-396-107, N1-396-140, 9-398-092, 9-302-075, 9-601-072). As noted above, Li & Fung's model was also featured prominently in John Hagel and John Seely Brown's book *The Only Sustainable Edge*. The company has been the focus of numerous articles in major magazines and newspapers.

5. Studies have found that almost half of strategic alliances fail. Companies with the best record of success have built dedicated capabilities for managing these alliances. See for example, Jeffrey H. Dyer, Prashant Kale and Harbir Singh, "How To Make Strategic Alliances Work," *Sloan Management Review*, Vol. 42, No. 4 (Summer 2001), pp. 37-43.

6. Although Thomas Friedman has compellingly captured a fundamental shift in the world, there is still considerable debate about this view of globalization that we also subscribe to—namely, that the world will become increasingly flat. Some question whether the world is headed in the direction of greater globalization, or, in Samuel Huntington's words, headed instead for a "clash of civilizations." Others in the anti-globalization movement question whether the flattening world is good thing and call for it to be stopped. Rising concerns about global warming and other environmental problems could also affect the flattening of the world. It is clear, as Friedman acknowledges, that the world is still not completely flat. Some of these different opinions ensure that there will not only be healthy debate for many years to come, but also that a variety of forces could slow or even reverse the flattening of the world.

7. "777 Family," www.boeing.com/commercial/777family/pf/pf_facts.html.

8. John Hagel and John Seely Brown introduced the term "process orchestrator" in their articles and book *The Only Sustainable Edge: Why Business Strategy Depends on Productive Friction and Dynamic Specialization* (Boston: Harvard Business School Press, 2005), based on Li & Fung's model. Earlier, Peter Drucker used the conductor and the orchestra to describe leadership with the flattening of the organization.

9. Ravi Aron and Jitendra V. Singh, "Getting Offshoring Right," *Harvard Business Review* Vol. 83, No. 12 (December 2005), pp. 135-143.

10. "Calling a Change in the Outsourcing Market: The Realities for the World's Largest Organizations," Deloitte Consulting (New York: April 2005).

11. Jeffrey H. Dyer, Prashant Kale, and Harbir Singh, "How to Make Strategic Alliances Work," *Sloan Management Review* Vol. 42, No. 4 (Summer 2001), 37.

12. Katie Hafner, "Growing Wikipedia Revises Its 'Anyone Can Edit' Policy," *New York Times*, 17 June 2006, http://select.nytimes.com/search/restricted/article?res=FB0611F83A550C748DDDAF0894DE404482.

13. Esquel Profile, http://www.esquel.com/en/index1.html; Barchi Peleg-Gillai "Esquel Group: Transforming Into a Vertically Integrated, Service-Oriented, Leading Manufacturer of Quality Cotton Apparel," Harvard Business School case study (#GS 48), January 20, 2006.

14. Benjamin Yen, Ali F. Farhoomand, Shamza Khan, "Polo Ralph Lauren & Luen Thai: Using Collaborative Supply Chain Integration in the Apparel Value Chain," (HKU595), November 24, 2006; "Global Supply Chain Solutions," *Wharton@Work*, July 2006, http://executiveeducation. wharton.upenn.edu/ebuzz/ 0607/thoughtleaders.html.

15. eBay press release, http://files.shareholder.com/downloads/ ebay/96892992x0x69405/2cbacae7-15cf-46fb-9a19-a89664d4e591/eBayIncEarningsReleaseQ42006.pdf.

16. "Two Millionth Passenger Vehicle Sold on eBay Motors," http://investor.ebay.com/releasedetail.cfm?ReleaseID=206868.

17. Thomas Friedman, *The World Is Flat: A Brief History of the 21st Century* (London: Allen Lane, 2005).

18. Oliver E. Williamson, *Markets and Hierarchies: Analysis and Antitrust Implications* (New York: Free Press, 1975).

19. James Surowiecki, *The Wisdom of Crowds: Why the Many Are Smarter Than the Few and How Collective Wisdom Shapes Business, Economies, Societies and Nations* (New York: Doubleday, 2004).

20. Ibid.

21. Howard Rheingold, *Smart Mobs: The Next Social Revolution* (New York: Basic Books, 2003).

22. Don Tapscott and Anthony D. Williams, *Wikinomics: How Mass Collaboration Changes Everything* (New York: Penguin Portfolio, 2006).

23. Tracy Staedter, "Open Source for the Open Road," *Fast Company*, March 2007, 36.

24. "Cost-Cutting Is Common but Not Critical in Outsourcing Decisions, Major Survey of Human Resources Executives Finds," The Bureau of National Affairs, Inc. (15 July 2004), www.bna.com/press/2004/outsource04.htm.

25. John Hagel and John Seely Brown introduced the term "process orchestrator" in their articles and book *The Only Sustainable Edge: Why Business Strategy Depends on Productive Friction and Dynamic Specialization* (Boston: Harvard Business School Press, 2005).

26. George S. Day and Paul J. H. Schoemaker, *Peripheral Vision: Detecting the Weak Signals That Will Make or Break Your Company* (Boston: Harvard Business School Press, 2006).

27. http://1worldcommunication.org/childlabor. htm#Pack%20(Un)happy%20Meal.

28. Ronald Alsop, "Perils of Corporate Philanthropy," *The Wall Street Journal,* January 16, 2002, http://www.harrisinteractive. com/services/pubs/PerilsOfPhilanthropy.pdf.

29. Peter F. Drucker, *The Practice of Management* (New York: Harper & Brothers Publishers, 1954).

30. Yoram Wind and Colin Crook, *The Power of Impossible Thinking: Transform the Business of Your Life and the Life of Your Business* (Upper Saddle River, NJ: Wharton School Publishing, 2004); and Roger Bannister, *The Four Minute Mile.* Guildford: The Lyons Press, 1981.

31. *Russell L. Ackoff, Jason Magidson, and Herbert J. Addison, Idealized Design: How to Dissolve Tomorrow's Crisis Today* (Upper Saddle River, NJ: Wharton School Publishing, 2006).

32. Rudolph Giuliani, *Leadership* (New York: Hyperion, 2002).

33. Eric Von Hipple, presentation to the International Academy of Management, New York City, 10 November 2005.

34. Chuck Salter, "Disruptors Welcome," *Fast Company,* May 2007, 92.

35. Larry Huston and Nabil Sakkab, "Connect and Develop: Inside Procter & Gamble's New Model for Innovation," *Harvard Business Review 84,* no. 3 (March 2006): 58–66.

36. McKinsey Quarterly 2002, no. 1.

37. "Build-A-Bear Workshop, Inc., Reports Fiscal 2006 Fourth Quarter and Full Year Results," http://phx.corporate-ir. net/phoenix.zhtml?c=182478&p=irol-newsArticle &ID=964723&highlight=.

38. "How to Hit a Moving Target," *Business Week* Online, www.businessweek.com/magazine/content/06_34/b3998423. htm?campaign_id=rss_null.

39. Steve Hamm with Nandini Lakshman, "The Trouble with India," *Business Week*, 19 March 2007, 48–58.

40. Anand Giridharadas, "India's Edge Goes Beyond Outsourcing," *The New York Times*, 4 April 2007, C-1.

41. www.answers.com/topic/c-a-5.

42. Goldman Sachs, "Dreaming with BRICS: The Path to 2050," Global Economics Paper No. 99, 2003. The original G6 formed in 1975 has been expanded to include Canada (G7) and Russia (G8).

43. "China's Retail Sector, 2005–2006, Part I: Market Developments and Trends," *Li & Fung Research Centre* 31, May 2006, 2.

44. Fara Warner, "The Rice-and-Noodles Mall," *Fast Company*, October 2006, 29.

45. Pietra Rivoli, *The Travels of a T-Shirt in the Global Economy* (John Wiley & Sons: Hoboken, NJ, 2006).

46. "The Business Week 50," *Business Week*, 26 March 2007: 74-90.

47. Gaurang Bhatia, "Olam International Limited," UBS Investment Research, 7 February 2007 and 28 November 2005.

48. Thomas L. Friedman, "Patient Capital for an Africa that Can't Wait," *The New York Times*, 20 April 2007, A-23.

49. Miguel Helfet, "Google, Master of Online Traffic, Helps Its Workers Beat the Rush," *The New York Times*, 10 March 2007, A-1.

50. Don Tapscott and Anthony D. Williams, *Wikinomics: How Mass Collaboration Changes Everything* (New York: Penguin Portfolio, 2006).

51. Robert Berner, "I Sold It Through the Grapevine," *Business Week*, 29 May 2006, www.businessweek.com/magazine/content/06_22/b3986060.htm?campaign_id=search.

52. S. Gordon Redding, *The Spirit of Chinese Capitalism* (Berlin: De Gruyter, 1990). He estimated that there were 40 million overseas Chinese in 1990.

53. Nicholas D. Kristof, "You, Too, Can Be Banker to the Poor," *The New York Times*, 27 March 2007, A-19.

54. www.womensworldbanking.org.

55. "ITT Fined $100 Million for Illegal Military Exports," Market Watch, www.marketwatch.com/news/story/itt-slapped-100-mln-penalty/story.aspx?guid=%7BFBA98C83-C8CD-4D33-B0D2-172CDB354944%7D.

56. Yoram Wind and Colin Crook, *The Power of Impossible Thinking: Transform the Business of Your Life and the Life of Your Business* (Upper Saddle River, NJ: Wharton School Publishing, 2004).

57. Vijay Mahajan and Kamini Banga, *The 86% Solution: How To Succeed in the Biggest Market Opportunity of the 21st Century* (Upper Saddle River, NJ: Wharton School Publishing, 2006).

58. C.K. Prahalad, *The Fortune at the Bottom of the Pyramid* (Upper Saddle River, NJ: Wharton School Publishing, 2004).

59. Yoram (Jerry) Wind and Vijay Mahajan, *Convergence Marketing: Strategies for Reaching the New Hybrid Consumer*, (Upper Saddle River, NJ: Financial Time/Prentice Hall, 2002).

60. Gary Hamel and C. K. Prahalad, "The Core Competence of the Corporation," *Harvard Business Review* 68, no. 3 (May–June 1990): 79–93.

INDEX

◫◫ Wharton School Publishing

In the face of accelerating turbulence and change, business leaders and policy makers need new ways of thinking to sustain performance and growth.

Wharton School Publishing offers a trusted source for stimulating ideas from thought leaders who provide new mental models to address changes in strategy, management, and finance. We seek out authors from diverse disciplines with a profound understanding of change and its implications. We offer books and tools that help executives respond to the challenge of change.

Every book and management tool we publish meets quality standards set by The Wharton School of the University of Pennsylvania. Each title is reviewed by the Wharton School Publishing Editorial Board before being given Wharton's seal of approval. This ensures that Wharton publications are timely, relevant, important, conceptually sound or empirically based, and implementable.

To fit our readers' learning preferences, Wharton publications are available in multiple formats, including books, audio, and electronic.

To find out more about our books and management tools, visit us at whartonsp.com and Wharton's executive education site, exceed.wharton.upenn.edu.

UNIVERSITY *of* PENNSYLVANIA

In five days, even Darwin would be shocked at how you've changed.

The Power of Impossible Thinking
Transform the Business of Your Life and the Life of Your Business
BY YORAM (JERRY) WIND AND COLIN CROOK

The Power of Impossible Thinking is about getting better at making sense of what's going on around you so you can make decisions that respond to reality, not inaccurate or obsolete models of the world. This bestseller reveals how mental models stand between you and the truth and how to transform them into your biggest advantage! Learn how to develop new ways of seeing, when to change to a new model, how to swap amongst a portfolio of models, how to understand complex environments, and how to do "mind R & D," improving models through constant experimentation.

ISBN 9780131877283, ©2006, 352 pp., $16.99 USA, $19.99 CAN

Selling Blue Elephants
How to Make Great Products That People Want BEFORE They Even Know They Want Them
BY HOWARD R. MOSKOWITZ, PH.D. AND ALEX GOFMAN

Can you remember the world before the iPod? How about the world before chunky tomato sauce or brown mustard? Many of these products came about not through focus groups and polling, but rather through research and development labs and marketers developing the products they knew customers would want, before customers knew they wanted them. Today your customers can actually help you create your next product. Rule Developing Experimentation (RDE) is a systematized process of designing, testing, and modifying alternative ideas, packages, products, or services in a disciplined way so that the developer and marketer discover what appeals to the customer, even if the customer can't articulate the need, much less the solution. Filled with real-life stories, this book will change the way people think about selling to their present and future customers.

ISBN 9780136136682, ©2007, 272 pp., $27.99 USA, $31.99 CAN